THE TRUTH ABOUT
SICKNESS AND HEALING

By

Donald McDowall

ISBN: 1-4107-8849-0 (e-book)
ISBN: 1-4107-8848-2 (Paperback)
ISBN: 1-4107-8847-4 (Dust Jacket)

Library of Congress Control Number: 2003095991

This book is printed on acid free paper.

Printed in the United States of America
Bloomington, IN

This book is not intended to replace medical advice.
If you are sick or suspect you are sick,
you should seek medical advice.

1stBooks – rev. 08/12/03

Also by Dr Donald Mcdowall

A Clinical Approach to Health Through Food Programming
Psychic Surgery – The Philippines Experience
Healing – Doorway to the Spiritual World
Clinical Pearls for Better Health
http://www.chiroclinic.com.au/pubs

To my wife, Annie, who sacrificed so much of her life and Strength to allow me the opportunity to find this knowledge.

FOREWORD

Down the ages people have sought to make sense of everyday, ordinary reality. Despite the best efforts of atheistic argument, human beings persist in the belief that there is a greater realm of being, a Self beyond the self, which many who have explored it have come to regard as the Real Reality. Every great religious belief system points to this possibility. The mystics dwell permanently in it and modern physics is reaching out ever more across the once great gulf that separated science and mysticism.

Mysticism is no longer the province of revered masters. All the great faiths were founded by great mystics – whether it be the authors of the Upanishads, or Buddha's experience under the Bo tree, or the Prophet's ascent with the Angel Gabriel or the Christ's preparation for his ministry. The mystical tradition has continued in the profound revelations of saints and holy people in every generation from Theresa of Avila to Ghandi, Hildegard of Bingen to Hafiz, Rumi to Krishnamurthi. These and others like them in every time and culture have been signposts to the direction of communion with the divine and the opportunity to transform the human experience into that peace which "passeth all understanding".

Enormous cultural shifts have taken place since the latter part of the 20th century. These include: accessibility of "New Age" approaches to the spiritual experience, the advent of mass communications and the decline of the authority of the main religions. These and other factors have conspired to provide a unique opportunity for more and more people to taste and validate the mystical experience. Enormous numbers of people are now willing to explore and own up to their mystical experiences including contact with the "spirits", channelling, ecstatic states and so on. Mysticism has been "proletarianised".

The enormity and variety of this experience is pregnant with the potential to transform the way we live in the world. But it also presents us with great challenges such as: How do we distinguish between the valid experience from that conjured up by the ego? How do we separate the true from the false revelation? How do we sort the offerings of wisdom from the seductions of seemingly high ideas rooted in the needs, conscious or unconscious, of the searcher?

The answers to these questions are not easy and can be uncomfortable to explore, but they demand attention from the earnest seeker. First of all we have the well-documented journeys of the great mystics, ancient and modern from all traditions, such as those I have mentioned above who have set the gold standard for the experience. They provide us with, among other things, a template against which to judge the deep from the shallow.

Secondly, we can trust our bullshit detectors, that common sense part of us, which prevents us from falling under the thrall of the seemingly wise person. No matter how profound his or her words seem to be, no matter how many books they publish, no matter how well they fix you with their steely eyes in that seminar or workshop; if something inside us is saying, this is nonsense – then pay attention to it!

Thirdly, we can listen to our hearts, that part of us which is deeply moved in us when we read or hear a truth and which helps us to isolate it from the false. Michael Harner, a man who has probably done more than any other to revive shamanism in Western culture, once said to me "Just because a spirit being is saying something doesn't mean it is true. Spirits, if we believe in them, may have limits to what they know too."

Fourthly, we can look beyond ourselves: to our mentors, priests, gurus and trusted wise teachers; to our communities of fellow seekers who can help us reflect upon and check out what is being offered.

Fifthly, we have an enormous body of literature and experience to draw upon where truth and the tools for identifying truth can be found. These include the sacred books of the world faiths to the oral traditions of native peoples and on into the scholarly texts and research now available. A defining treatise on this theme is the work of Evelyn Underhill as described in her book "Mysticism". It is regarded internationally as a classic. Our documented works are a rich resource for the testing of truth.

"The Truth about Sickness and Healing-The Observer's Point of View" falls within the heritage of those who have sought to write down their experiences that do not lend themselves to rational analysis. Indeed, the rationalists will have a field day on a book like this, as they always do. Revelation and mysticism are not the province of reason but of experience. Wisdom comes when we work with that experience to seek truth. Is there truth here? I must leave the reader to be the judge of that.

There is a storehouse of ideas to explore here that we can sit with and test out and challenge and reflect upon. Like other recent texts in the genre, such as Walsch's "Conversations with God" or Rodegast and Stanton's "Emmanuel" series, insights and questions are offered which often beg more questions and more searching. That is perhaps as it should be. The world is full of people and things telling us what to think and do.

One of the qualities of books like Donald's is that in the end they leave the reader to make the decisions, and that lies at the heart of spiritual empowerment. There is dogma aplenty offered these days, sometimes forced upon, the spiritual seeker. Writings that question and inform are the stuff, the grist for the mill, of a maturing spirituality – God knows the world needs it.

Prof. Steve Wright FRCN, MBE
St. Martins College, Lancaster, UK
Editor: Sacred Space-The International Journal
Exploring Spirituality and Health.

INTRODUCTION

My friend, Donald McDowall, has really gone a long way. Beginning as a chiropractor concerned mainly with the physical manipulation of the body, he has now graduated to working with the mind and spirit of patients as well.

But Donald has always been curious about the unseen world from the very beginning, only he did not have the means to access this, until he met his perfect mate in the person of Annie, a Filipino clairvoyant psychologist in the Philippines. Together they explored the mysteries of the spirit world and how spirits interface with the physical world.

This book, which this couple has written with the help of their spirit guides, is a valuable contribution to the growing and expanding literature of channelled messages from the spirit world. It contains practical tips ranging from such mundane concerns as headaches and migraines, to how to work with spirits themselves.

Reading Donald and Annie McDowall's manuscript, "The Truth about Sickness and Healing – The Observer's Point of View", reminds me of the classic work of Allan Kardec. In his two great books "Spirits Book" and "The Book of Mediums", Allan Kardec obtained answers about the spirit world from the spirits themselves. Donald and Annie have done the same for the contemporary world. They directly asked the spirits for answers to questions that have interested modern man for a long time, such as, how do spirits communicate with humans? Why do they have to use mediums? Why do some healings fail? How do we protect ourselves from the evil spirits? How does healing take place? And many, many more!

I am glad that Donald and Annie have taken pains to record faithfully the communications they have been having with the spirits so that these can be shared with a greater number of people who are hungry for this knowledge.

I believe the next phase of human evolution will take place in the area of consciousness. It is happening now. Such books as this will help in the expansion of man's consciousness and accelerate his evolution.

I congratulate and salute the works of Donald and Annie in this direction. I am happy to have been instrumental in bringing these two lovely individuals together. With their work they are helping to bring healing to the mind, body and spirit of an entire world.

JAIME T. LICAUCO
Author, Journalist and
Metaphysical Researcher,
Makati, Philippines.

AUTHOR'S INTRODUCTION

This series of books describes the understanding I gained as Annie and I explored the contact we had established with our spirit teachers.

In 1994 I completed my last visit to the Philippines, gathering information to help me understand the power of the healers who practiced there as psychic surgeons, magnetic healers and spiritual healers. The proofs of God's work through these healers had re-established my faith and encouraged me to search deeper within myself for an understanding of my mission in life and the extent of my healing abilities. In that process I met Annie. Annie, a psychologist and Montessori teacher travelled with me on many of those journeys. Her gift as a medium for these teachers gave me a direct contact to messengers of God.

I now had a wonderful opportunity with Annie to explore questions that had plagued my mind and heart through my life. Questions about my professional practice, my family problems, the communities difficulties, the prospect of the future, the reality of earth changes, UFOs and the reality of ETs, as well as some of the more ancient questions regarding the validity of the Bible, its stories and its pertinence to the problems of today.

Between 1994, up to and including 1997, I recorded on tape all the meditations and conversations which took place with these teachers. These conversations were recorded for their value, not only to Annie and myself, but also to others who were interested in answers to the same questions. These tapes were transcribed and edited for the relevant topics that will be published in this series of books.

I suppose the initial haunting question for me as a chiropractor, which led to my search for more knowledge about healing, was why some people got better and others, who received the same attention, were slower to respond. The essence of this first book includes the answers I received to those questions. It had always intrigued me why a miraculous cure could take place for one person and the same opportunities for cure would have no effect on another person.

The spirit teachers very patiently took me through the kindergarten understanding of how the human body expresses the strength of the spiritual nature of the person, through the primary school, high school, college, and now in the graduate phase of understanding the subtleties of nature and the awesome influence of God as He provides opportunity for man's development.

I have always believed in God. But my faith in churches and religions was tested, and often shattered, when I sought help for answers to these questions from other people about the realities of life. As I travelled around the world, I would often visit churches of every denomination. In many countries the edifices were beautiful, ornate and a tribute to the engineers who constructed them, and the finances of the population who funded them. Yet often they were empty of the very people they were supposed to serve. They were often seen as monuments with historical significance and now had an absence of spiritual purpose. I had come to the conclusion that churches and religions taught people to pray, but rarely explained how to listen for the answers.

From this point of view, these books may not say anything earth shattering to the reader, but may simply provide an awareness of the small things that are often missed, similar to the power of blades of grass to grow in the cracks of a footpath, or the grains of sand that strengthen the concrete between the bricks. These are insignificant yet imperative to the integrity of the structure and the power of life.

The meditations Annie and I were involved in were sometimes planned, where we would pray and ask for help and the teachers would arrive and speak. Sometimes there would be three or four teachers of different ranking at the one meditation, answering questions topical to their expertise. Sometimes the negative entities were allowed to come to teach me the contrast and the reality that is often ignored, of evil influences.

Our meditation sessions would last from a few minutes, if instruction was given to us to prepare for a particular event that would come, to three or four hours where I had a multitude of questions. Generally the meditations usually began about one or two in the morning, when both Annie and I were asleep, and the teacher would speak through Annie, wake me up and then we would discuss the questions in my mind. The teacher preferred this time; he said it was when my mind was free of cobwebs. I found that I often had to rest at work during lunchtime or in the afternoons in order to maintain this schedule. Annie would be just as tired as me and have to rest afterwards. As a trance-medium, she had no recollection of any of the experiences that took place, other than fatigue.

Later I would recognise the teacher speaking through Annie when there was no obvious meditation, but a necessity on the part of the teacher to inform us of a particular event. Similarly, Annie would have no memory of the discussion, other than a time shift. The request of the spiritual teachers was always to encourage us to rest and build our strength – physically, mentally and emotionally – to cope with the demands of these instructions. Choices were always given as to whether we wished to continue or not.

I took full advantage of these experiences to ask all the questions that came into my mind, to satisfy the reality of my experience; often testing and proving what the teachers were telling me.

Many situations took place where I began to recognise God's influence through other people. Sometimes we would be at a Buddhist monastery, or a Catholic or Protestant church, and the minister would be prompted to present the answer to the question that was in my mind at the time. It seemed to me that these teachings gradually enabled me to see the reality of the work of God's messengers around me. Often these influences were so subtle, they were very easy to miss.

The reader should desire to peruse this material for answers to similar questions.

I have no desire to begin a church or a following with this information. It was presented to Annie and I to help us find our missions, our purpose together, and our future. Now I understand the answers to these questions. It provides an example for others to find true meaning in their lives without dependency upon a financial or political structure, where they might become abused, delayed or side tracked.

The secret to understanding God is awareness and the art of subtle listening. Some of us have to have a tap on the shoulder to get our attention; others learn more quickly. I have learned the hard way to understand these lessons and now appreciate the gentleness and power with which God does His work.

CONTENTS

THE WORLD OF INTELLIGENCE IN WHICH WE LIVE.

How does our world function and who is God? Probably the best place to start answering these questions is with man's perception of God. History records God in the eyes of the beholder. Each description varies according to the beliefs, intelligence and education of the writer.

My understanding of the word "God" is that it encompasses the intelligence in which all matter exists and communicates. God encompasses all genders and incorporates all expressions of life. God's expression of love was to create man and his environment. The purpose of which is to provide individuals with opportunities for development of character. God provides an example of balance, love and harmony that we can choose to constantly aspire to amidst the distractions of our life.

God has created and appointed leaders to administer his work. These intelligences are referred to from our perspective as masters or angels. They have been tested for their loyalty. They exercised their choice of doing things God's way or their own way. They either assist lesser intelligences to learn more about God and become closer to the harmony of God or distract from this purpose. With God's permission these masters can access any of his creations to express and communicate his purpose. The negative masters encourage rejection of God and pride in the misery of themselves and others.

The Masters are assisted by Senior Guides. These guides are intelligences that have had a series of human experiences and instructional experiences from their guides and have completed their tasks. They carry out the instructions from the Masters and report to them.

The Senior Guides are assisted by junior ranking intelligences whom have progressed through the human experience and can pass on this knowledge to humans working on their next ranking. These guides

1

are often experienced in specific areas of discipline and character. They will work with their student through inspiration and awareness until they can pass on their subject to the next guide. They may attend the subject for a specific purpose or assist through the whole development of a period similar to a schoolteacher with a student. By doing this, the guide is increasing his ranking according to the success of his subject and the methods through which he has permission to communicate.

Some intelligences inhabit non human bodies. These bodies may consist of light or other forms of matter. Some bodies are genetically constructed to suit our atmosphere. We refer to these as Extra-Terrestrial. They also contribute to the human school of our life by injecting their knowledge of using matter. Some live on this planet. Some come from other planets. They can live in adjacent dimensions in the same time as us. They understand the perspective of our planet and our knowledge. They are under the direction of the Masters.

Not every disincarnate spirit becomes a guide. Those who cannot accept their death and feel cheated in their life remain on the planet until they realize what has happened to them and choose to move on. They can learn to manipulate matter and create difficulties for their antagonists. We call them Ghosts.

Most disincarnate spirits accept the results of their lives, leave the material world and meet guides who were their teachers. They study the experience they have had as humans until they recognise the next lessons or character traits they need to learn. They then wait for the right opportunity in the right environment with the right parents to manifest so they can return or reincarnate. The selection is not of their choosing but of the teachers who have assisted them this far. They can accept or reject this opportunity.

Some humans have connected with their spiritual purpose and provide a more direct communication between the two worlds. These we consider channels or mediums. The messages they give may come from the guides of both extremes. Some are regarded as prophets, but many just quietly go about their business helping others.

We are regarded by these other intelligences as "concrete people". This perspective appears to be in relationship to the speed at which our material world functions. The slowness of the physical body is compared to the speed of thought of these intelligences. Hence their communication with us is via thought forms and impressions. Each person will be sensitive to these messages in different ways according to the sensitivity of their nervous system or emotions.

Natural human intelligence is instinctive in nature, similar to other species. Humans are born with genetic abilities including reproductive, communicative and survival skills. Other skills appear to progressively develop with the experiences of each generation. The genetic pool is improved or damaged according to the contribution of the previous generation. This genetic construct is observed by the guides and used to choose appropriate birth families. These families provide the most useful bodies, minds and environments for the predetermined missions of the assigned intelligences.

Once incarnate, our intelligence adapts to our bodies and environment. This adaptation develops our character and personality. In this way we become who we are meant to be with the physical tools we need for our work. If we become distracted from our missions and fail to use our opportunities for their right purpose then we are taken out of our human form to reassess what went wrong and wait for another opportunity to incarnate with a modified mission. This is the purpose of life.

THE TEACHERS IN THIS BOOK

Spirit Guides are highly evolved intelligences that do not have physical bodies.

While guides are generally hesitant to have names, they find it is easier to identify with humans by their character. Guides are generally acknowledged between themselves according to a ranking of responsibility. This appears to give them an energy code expressed physically as a colour.

Mathew was the first guide I became aware of. The healer made me aware of him during a discussion one night in Baguio, Philippines. We had difficulty communicating.

Acton began communicating in meditation sessions while I was in the Philippines. His purpose was to give me more information about my destiny.

Lucas was the next guide who came. His responsibility was to provide more detailed information about aspects of healing, as well as the preparation of patients to receive healing. He seemed to have some familiarity with the incarnation of Luke in the New Testament.

Paul appeared to be more an academic, with information regarding the scriptural context of questions I asked, dealing with different religions. He also was familiar with the character of Paul in the New Testament.

Zechariah worked with me at the same time as Lucas, Paul and Jonah. His job was more related to the physical manifestations of healing, both in the patient and in the healer. These changes enabled the healer to be more adaptable to the spiritual energy needed to help the patient. In essence his job was to heal the healer, on a physical level.

Jonah was the supervisor of the previous guides and often called on them to answer questions on their specialty, yet supervised their contributions. He explained that his last incarnation brought him to a realisation of enlightenment. His friends have recorded a fragment of this work as *"The Practice of the Presence of God-Conversations and Letters of Brother Lawrence"* first published in 1692, reprinted in 1993 by Oneworld Publications, Oxford.

Master Gordon is one of four masters that supervise the inhabitants of the earth. His responsibilities involve the progressive development of enlightenment in our species. All the previous guides were under his direction. His authority dominates the negative entities and spirits. His influence permeates groups of people. His instructions are more disciplined and strict. He takes orders directly from God.

Solomon is a novice in the affairs of the human world. He is a guide under the direct instruction of Master Gordon. His purpose is to teach compassion and sense the current attitude of human life, in preparation for incarnation.

Alexander is an assistant to Solomon and learns, in an apprentice format, about the responsibilities of human life.

ES (Evil Spirit): in general a definition was not made as to the name of the entity involved in some of the meditations. However, his power was exemplified by the ease with which he took over some of the meditations and came into conflict with the guides. Master Gordon has power over him. He is also referred to throughout this discussion as Lucifer, Satan, the Devil, the Evil One, and Angel of Death etc.

WHERE THE MEDITATIONS TOOK PLACE

The conversations for this book were recorded during meditations in the Philippines and Australia.

Philippines: Manila and Baguio (north of Manila) on the island of Luzon..

Australia: Canberra, Australian Capital Territory; Uluru, Northern Territory; Adelaide, South Australia; Melbourne, Victoria.

THE SEQUENCE OF CHAPTERS
AND CONTENT OF THE TITLES

The topics have been arranged in the order they were received. While it may, at times appear confusing to find similar titles later in the book and not grouped together, the information received often clarifies and expands on the earlier knowledge.

I have titled each discussion according to my understanding of its message; however, the reader should understand that each discussion has many messages, both written and unwritten. These will be interpreted according to the reader's perspective and awareness.

THE CONTENT OF THE NEW BOOKS

The following discussions describe the purpose of these books.

Donald: How many books will I be preparing?

Jonah: The three books we refer to have already been divided. The first book is about your beliefs, your encounters. The second concerns the teachings you have learned. The third is your journey.

D: I understand.

J: The journey includes your guide. Presently you can focus on the first. There will be more to come for the second book. The third book is still in limbo.

D: I understand that.

J: Other people should not interpret the way we explain things to you. The book should be written as is. The essence should be intact.

D: I understand.

J: I know you can't see it yet but this book will encompass the world. That is why we trust you with that.

J: As a man you are limited, physically and cannot reach everybody. These books will spread the word of God, especially to those unhappy with their lives.

D: Some people will say the Bible is enough.

J: You cannot force a person to believe, to change the colour of his skin. You would be surprised how many question the Bible. There have been many books written about the Bible and its weaknesses.

D: There are other Scriptures as well, such as the Koran, or the Book of Mormon, or other revelations that have come through guides to different people.

J: These have helped. Still there are people wanting more illumination. The needs of those before are different from this generation.

D: I understand what you mean. A different culture is developing in western countries.

J: People in eastern countries are also questioning their books and their beliefs. This book is non-denominational and for everybody. We do not speak of any particular religion here, but of our relationship with God, with the Supreme Being.

D: Many books are written by guides through their channels and have been published. Hundreds are in the library. How will our book be different?

J: You question us?

D: You know I am interested in details. You mentioned the second book would involve teaching, but more information would need to be given.

J: Have you not yet formulated how this should be written? Like two people conversing. Like a student and a teacher seated together and conversing. Like two people discussing something. That is the way this should be done.

D: I understand that.

J: There should not be a textbook texture to these books.

D: Awareness is very high. People are very interested in taking self-responsibility.

Donald McDowall

THE NEXT BOOK

Master Gordon: The next book should be ready soon, for people to better understand what is happening around them. There are those who still do not understand the meaning of life, why they are here, why they feel what they feel. They do not understand how to react properly. The book will be of great help to these people. It will be helpful also to those who understand but who need something to hold on to, to strengthen themselves in their journeys.

This book should help people understand themselves.

WHY PEOPLE GET SICK

Paul: What is in your heart Donald? Why do you get sick?

D: Maybe because I work too hard?

P: Is that the only reason you get sick?

D: I ask myself that same question many times.

P: In my experience with other people, they absorb, in some degree, negative vibrations given off by others around them. You should learn to be more discreet and not absorb everything like a sponge.

You should not be very adventurous; even your friend, the healer, has told you to be very careful and discriminating.

D: I try to be careful and search for the truth.

P: Just because it is there, you should be careful what you absorb. Many things are disguised as truth.

Does it follow that everything served you, you should taste? Of course not. You should be very careful.

How would you know if the food served before you is poisoned? The food looks good, smells good and maybe will also taste good. But inside your body, the food can create poison and kill you.

D: What can I do to protect myself?

P: Think positively all the time. In that capacity, I find Annie more advanced than you. She has learned to steel herself from negative thoughts. Spiritually she is stronger than you. Draw from that strength, her reserved strength, because she is one of the most faithful people we have encountered, not only physically, but in her thoughts as well. Try to be faithful.

D: I feel that too, which is why I like to be with her.

P: That is the journey that every human has. And that is how we learn.

D: How can I prepare my body so it will become stronger and not get so sick?

P: Be faithful in your thoughts. Do not punish yourself *[Reflecting over past mistakes]*.

THE SOURCE OF MIRACLES

Paul: A man, a human being, cannot perform miracles by himself. He needs God and needs his spirit guides to help him carry out his mission. That is what you have been doing. You are now doing it right.

D: What can I do to become stronger with the energy?

P: Be faithful to yourself; be faithful to your beliefs, to your trust in God. Learn to focus, as Annie has been telling you. Focus and do not let your mind wander, especially when you are healing.

D: I have been trying to focus more. Do you see improvement?

P: Just keep yourself faithful. You know what I mean by that. Always keep your mind and your heart clean. We are not talking of just the physical here. Focusing your mind is vital.

HEALING TECHNIQUES

Paul: When you are healing people, just concentrate on their illnesses. After that, switch off. Otherwise, you will not have much energy left. Learn to do that. What negativities you take away from them, seal in a mental container. Do you understand?

D: Yes.

P: That will help.

DO NOT ABSORB NEGATIVITY

Paul: Do not get involved personally or sympathise with your patients, and do not absorb the negativities in them. This patient you have asked about has a lot of negativities. You must lift them from his shoulders, but at the same time do not get involved. Learn to balance the two. Absorbing negativities will again weaken your body as well as your soul, and that is not good. This is a first step in your test.

Donald McDowall

FOCUSING ENERGY

Paul: In the past you have asked how to strengthen your power. You are again not focusing; this can be exhausting. Especially when you pay attention one minute and not the next.

D: How do you see me not paying attention?

P: You should learn to build up your energy. When you go to new and different places, you use up the energy you are trying to build, you are de-focusing yourself. A foreign place easily sways you into exotic things. How do you know that the Devil is not waiting for you there in disguise?

D: Are you saying to visit friends I have known for many years, who have skills I find helpful is not right for me?

P: I did not say that. What I am saying is the extra places you want to go to, the extra people you want to meet will not do you any good. Meeting friends who have helped you before is okay.

Let your heart decide for you. When we say look out for the whore we do not mean a physical whore. Do not be swayed by the Devil dressed in fine clothes. Do not be swayed into believing something that is not real.

D: I am learning more about the importance of this awareness.

P: There are some places you can explore, but we are warning you to be very careful. There will be some exotic places you will visit which will attract your fancy. Like the fool's gold that looks like gold, but is not gold; do you understand? You should learn to be discriminating. Sometimes you are fooled, I am sorry to say.

D: That is why I am trying to learn more, so I do not have that problem.

Some of my friends are very spiritual. One of my teachers gets instruction from time to time. He keeps this very much to himself.

P: You can trust your friends to a certain degree. But not everything that they teach you, not everything that they share with you is for your good. Do not absorb everything; choose only that which will help you in your development. Be faithful. That is your weakness; sometimes you experiment. That is not very good. It is like a teenager experimenting with marijuana; they feel good with the first puffs, so they try again, and again. This makes them feel good, so they take another puff and feel better, until they are hooked. Then they try something harder. So we are telling you to be faithful, do not experiment on something you should not touch.

THE BATTLE FOR HEALTH

D: Why does my body have so many aches and pains?

Acton: Number one, you work beyond your body's capabilities.

Number two, you empathise and absorb negative energy from your patients and friends.

Number three; you still have doubts about yourself.

Now you get the solutions. We have discussed and itemised these so you can work on them.

WHY BODIES SUFFER PAIN

Lucas: The physical comes from the spiritual. If you have no spiritual gift, you will not get a physical gift, because of not being worthy, not deserving. This is up to you. We have armed you with your gifts. Use them properly. But still we cannot insist.

D: You said you have armed me. This seems like I am going into battle.

L: Every day is a battle for you. Every day is a battle for man. There are those who are very much prepared and there are those who go to battle without preparing. When we say we are arming you, it is for the enemy that is the disease of the soul and the body. That is your battle every day.

D: Yesterday we had many battles, as you predicted. There were many people with doubts and problems.

L: Did you doubt me?

D: No, you were very clear. I got very tired, even though I saw only a few people.

L: Learn not to absorb their problems. Help them solve their problems, but do not absorb these problems.

Donald McDowall

MEDITATING AND DEVELOPING FOCUS

Lucas: Every afternoon you can meditate. Jonah will be there to teach you how to focus, because that is what you lack.

D: I have been trying to understand more about the word focus.

L: You being one in mind with the Supreme Being. That is focusing.

D: This is becoming easier to do.

L: We notice you are developing faster now.

HOW TO FOCUS

D: Tell me about focus and the healing power. Does focus mean to be able to be one with God and to merge my soul with God?

Lucas: Yes, to be able to give yourself to Him when you are about to heal. Let Him run your body. Let Him direct your body. Be like a puppet to Him. Let Him work inside you, through you, with you. That is what focusing means. Focus on God.

THE SKILLS OF EDGAR CAYCE

D: I am interested in understanding how Edgar Cayce used to work as a healer.

Lucas: Let us talk of Edgar Cayce.

Not everything he did was written. He also misfired. When you write a book about a person you analyse the best the person has done. A spirit guide has limits too.

The physical body limits every human. Even you are limited, but as you move forward, you will increase your knowledge, power and gifts.

D: That will be very helpful. I would like to be able to do that.

JESUS HEALING AS CHIROPRACTOR

Lucas: I believe Jesus was the first chiropractor.

D: How was that?

L: He was setting bones.

D: I thought the ancient Egyptians set bones.

L: Yes, but he was the first known chiropractor; although at the time there was no name for this. The term chiropractor was coined only recently.

D: Did he teach you these things?

L: No, he did not.

D: I want to know more about how Jesus worked as a chiropractor.

Jonah [J]: Did you not read this in the Bible? He could make the blind see.

D: Did he do that by working with the spine?

J: Yes, by manipulation. You will learn that, and, in some ways, your guide will show you how.

D: I thought he spat in the dirt on his hand and put the spittle into the eye.

J: This is in the Bible, that is true. But how can spittle cure the blind? People need to see props. Jesus used props because in his time, when he was healing these people, non-believers as well as believers watched him. They could not understand that massaging and stroking could straighten out the human body. He has to use a prop to make

23

them believe. There are instances when he did the same thing in his own hometown and he was not believed. They thought he was a quack.

JESUS AS A HEALER

D: You told me that Jesus was a chiropractor.

Lucas: Are you having a problem with that?

D: I was surprised. I know the skill is very old and has gone through many traditions. But I was interested to know that he physically manipulated bodies and used his skills like that instead of just praying or snapping his fingers.

L: If you read the Bible very carefully you will understand better. He made the cripple walk. This was not pointing a finger at the limb and telling the person to straighten up and walk. He had to manipulate bones, muscles and nerves. He, of course, has something special because he is God. There should always be a logical, rational explanation about what happens. That which cannot be explained rationally is a miracle.

D: So he did not do miracles all the time?

L: He has to use the body. If he only wants to perform miracles, I do not think he will be able to hold people's faith, or their trust in him. People will start thinking he is from the Devil. So people have to know and see things done rationally. Do you understand? That is why God has to use a human body to relate to man.

D: That is why focus is so important.

L: If you can learn to do that, you are home free.

GIFT OF HEALING

D: I am trying hard. I wonder why the power has to be transferred. Why it is not just given as a grace.

Zechariah: This is not given to everybody.

D: Is the healing power rationed amongst healers?

Z: No, you do not understand. Not everybody is given the task of healing people the way some healers do. Now, as we have said, this is a special gift bestowed on man to help mankind. One healer asked for this power. We taught him the way because we saw the pureness of his intention. Now you have requested the same. This man is starting to lose his touch because of the worldly things he does. Now you, on the other hand, are discovering your spiritual power because you are learning to centre your life on important issues. As you do that, you gain more power and increase your energy. That is what we meant by granting and taking away. This is a special gift one can have, by giving up some material pleasures.

D: Have I given up enough?

Z: You have to learn to centre your desire in one place.

HOW TO CENTRE ONE'S SELF

Zechariah: You do everything and you are everywhere. That is not a complaint, but you have to keep your thoughts together. Keep yourself together.

D: What is the best way to do that?

Z: Number one – have more time for meditation. That is very important. Jonah has discussed that.

Number two – what are your priorities?

Number three – do not be everything. Just choose what you really want to be.

D: What do you mean by that?

Z: Well, you counsel a lot. You deal in business. You play too. Three aspects of your life have been projected in the last few days, and, of course, you are a family man too.

Let us focus on your work. You do not budget your energy for your work. Learn to budget, because if you do not, you will only have a little to yourself and will not be able to meditate more. When you hit the bed, you fall asleep instantly. How can we communicate with you if you are always tired? I am not saying that you should not help people. No, your work is to help them, but do not go out of your way to give more than you are capable of. You should leave some energy for yourself and your immediate family.

IMPROVING YOUR HEALING ABILITY

Jonah: We have only scratched the surface. There is more. Be patient. In getting there, you become more sensitive to what is going on, more analytical and that is good. This means you are concentrating more, that you are focusing more. Continue with your meditation. Do this every day.

D: Before I go to the next step, I have to strengthen my body. Doing this kind of meditation is more demanding. Will you tell me when I am ready for the next step or will this just happen?

J: Even surgeons have specialisations. They train for that; like a bone surgeon, a heart surgeon, and so on. They specialise. We are going to train you to do something specific. Before you can do that, you have to strengthen your body because you will be using a lot of energy. That is why we do not want you to spend all your energy at once. Learn to budget and distribute your energy so that at the end of each day you still have some for yourself.

D: Am I doing better now?

J: Just a little; although sometimes you need a little tap to get you to stop.

D: I feel that now.

J: Sometimes the energy you exert is wasted. That is not good.

D: I always thought one could never give too much to a person because they will always be helped.

J: The patient should take only what they need. Because if they do not, it will not be used by the body and is just wasted. Learn to distribute and budget your energy well.

THE TRUTH ABOUT SICKNESS AND HEALING

REQUIREMENTS FOR HEALERS

Jonah: This other healer you know is lower in ranking because he cannot even control himself. He is doing the side roads. Healers should not have vices. They should remain pure. That is the reason why healers die young. They have to be taken out because when a human being misuses his gift, it becomes dangerous; not only to himself, but also for the people he touches.

Now, these guides should be strong enough to discipline the persons they are guiding. That is why I am rather strict with you because I want you to progress towards your goal. I want you to succeed, not only for you, but also for the people whose lives you will touch, as a healer. That is why we keep telling you to be faithful. Honour your commitments.

Donald McDowall

BE CAREFUL WHEN MEDITATING WITH OTHERS

Jonah: In the morning when you meditate at the healing clinic, you do not have to understand what is being said, but you can feel the energy flowing among the people. The energy is not that strong because all these people you are with are very weak in the body. Most of them have not been in touch with their spirits lately. Only now are they getting acquainted with their spiritual world. You do not have to go with that flow. You can transcend that, but need to be with them too. They can use some of your energy while they are praying and meditating.

USING ENERGY WISELY

Jonah: Your friend will have another message. If he does not pay attention, that is his loss. Zechariah came to him so he could help you. Zechariah came to him to prepare him for the transition that would be abruptly taken from him. You will feel your energy flowing stronger and stronger. Do not misuse this energy. If you see somebody needing help, do not use up all your energy. No. Conserve your energy now. We will tell you the right time to start using it. You have to build up your energy. You should not feel that it is your duty to help each person you see now. Remember other healers are there. So what you should do is conserve energy.

D: One of the healers asked me to try and use energy with the other people. I have not done that yet.

J: No, not yet. You will, but not yet. We will give you the sign when to start using your energy. You are just regaining your lost energy. This is not extra energy; this is just the energy you have used which we are giving back to you. This energy if used now will diminish and you will feel weak.

31

WHAT HAPPENS DURING SLEEP?

D: I noticed you took me out of my body while I was sleeping. When I woke up I could see all these other people around me.

Jonah: What people?

D: It was like a classroom. Is that right?

J: I took you to your training. Whenever you sleep – we have discussed this! Whenever a human being sleeps the spirit chooses to stay inside the body or go out to school for some lessons in the spiritual world. We have discussed that haven't we?

D: Yes, I understand that. It was the first time, though, that I have been conscious of it.

J: Is that good or bad for you?

D: I wanted to be conscious of it, so it was good for me. Usually I can sleep, I do not wake up, but this time I kept having experiences and being aware of them.

ACCEPTING GIFTS OF THE SPIRIT

D: I have a headache from the meditation yesterday. I did not mean to be greedy. I did not want to waste my time. I wanted to be able to go as far as I could. Are you happier with my progress?

Jonah: I am happy with your progress, but your attitude is not so good.

D: I have tried to change. What are you concerned about?

J: What you were saying just now. You might have indigestion.

D: Why?

J: Why! You should not eat all the food just because it is served on the table. You should be selective. Choose well; do not grab whatever is there. Perhaps these are other people's leftovers.

D: What do you mean?

J: Like energy that might be negative. You must be more discriminating.

D: Is that what I did?

J: Yes. You were picking up all the things that you see on the road. You should not do this. I let you do this for the experience. If everything you picked was right, this would be a wonderful experience. You would not have headaches or other symptoms.

You should be discriminating. Select your food, do not just grab what is on the table. You know well how to combine these. Apply this same process to energy.

D: I was trusting that you would expose me to what I needed. So I was not thinking.

J: I did expose you, but I did not expect you to grab everything.

D: I was very excited.

J: I know. That is why we let you. That is another lesson learned. Next time be more selective.

A CAUSE OF HEADACHES

D: Why do I have this headache?

Jonah: This is lesson number two. That is another reason why you had a headache. You gave too much energy.

D: Some of these people were very sick.

J: I know, but the energy that you projected, the energy that you exerted, was far too much, leaving you depleted. We are discussing this clinically. Without enough energy you are defenceless and become exposed to negativities.

Donald McDowall

USING THE ENERGY

D: Thank you. How do you see the changes in my skills now?

Jonah: Your skills are sharper, more powerful and precise. Except for one thing: when you start working, you do not know when to put on the brake. You are a cautious car driver, but with your energy and healing power, you do not know when to step on the brake.

D: I was trusting to be prompted when to stop or to change, so I try to wait until I feel that.

J: Waiting, waiting, waiting can sometimes cause accidents. You do not need somebody beside you. Don't you call these back-seat drivers?

D: I am just learning to drive this energy.

J: We understand. Now we are analysing this. Be selective when you sympathise. You asked, that is why we are explaining, analysing. We are not here to put you down, but to show you your weak points, so we can work on that together.

HOW PHYSICAL PAIN AFFECTS THE SOUL

Jonah: Pain is having an effect on this patient's body. Her body is in agony. That is why she is suffering those cramps. That is why she is having problems. This is hard work for the soul.

D: I have not heard that before.

J: When the body is in agony, the soul is affected as well.

D: What is the remedy?

J: Stronger faith. You see people using this when they are fire walking.

D: Yes.

J: Her life is a struggle to prepare her for what is to come. Your life is also a struggle, to toughen you also for what is to come. I have struggles, too, to be a more effective teacher. I hope everything I have said does not go in vain.

Donald McDowall

THE TIME FOR REST

Jonah: We will always be there for you, but there are times when we have to let you undergo experiences to make you learn.

D: Sometimes I like to have a rest.

J: The only time a person can rest is when he is dead.

D: You are very harsh, Jonah.

J: That is life. Life is tough.

CASINOS AND NEGATIVE PLACES

D: We visited a casino today while at our conference; the atmosphere is not really very nice, we stayed only a few minutes.

Jonah: Did you abuse that opportunity?

D: I do not believe so. We watched the people. As soon as Annie felt her throat becoming irritated, we left.

J: This is not her ground, nor your ground. Lots of negativities are there.

D: I understand.

J: Stay away from places like that. These are not for you; unless you want to be like them.

D: I think making a contrast is important when we are learning.

J: If that is the way you think, but what if you are in one of your depressed moods and you go to places like that; you would be swallowed whole by the negativities there.

WHY WE GET ILL

D: Is that why my body has been getting sicker, because I have so many visitors?

Jonah: Do not blame the spirits, Donald. Your body gets sick because of the negativities you absorbed in your past, and even now.

D: I have tried to stop them and to change them.

J: Do your best. Associate with like spirits, with like people. Associating with people with unlike feelings and vibrations is not good for you.

D: I understand that.

J: That is it. That is why you get sick. You should put a limit on what you can absorb. Why do you keep junk in your house? You throw it away. That is why you have your big bins outside the house, for the junk. You do not keep junk in your bedroom. Why keep junk inside your soul?

THE QUALITY OF HEALERS

D: How do you diagnose our problems?

Master Gordon: We put a magnifying glass on your wife and analyse each part of her. We get in the mind and the heart. We see the rippling; we see the deficiency inside her.

D: This is what Edgar Cayce did with his patients.

MG: Who is Edgar Cayce?

D: He was a psychic during the 1940s. He was very famous because he could go to sleep and then look inside patients' bodies and see what they needed. He would be guided to give the prescriptions that would help them[1].

MG: That is very interesting.

D: He received a lot of information and was very famous for his work.

MG: So, it is very much like one of us.

D: Do you have someone like that who works with healers?

MG: There are many of us who work with healers.

D: I know there are some psychics in South America who work like that. There was one called Arigo, and a Dr Fritz who was the spirit guide of Arigo[2]. He could do psychic surgery with a knife or his hands and other instruments. He was called the surgeon with the rusty knife, because people never got sick and he was always able to help them. He always knew the new drugs even before these were marketed. I studied his work. This was very interesting. I have tried to study many psychics[3].

MG: Not all healers are from God. There are copycats who are very impressive.

D: How can you tell the difference? They both seem to do good for people.

MG: On the surface, yes. Just like gold-plated jewellery; only on the surface. They try to draw people into believing in them. Once they have their beliefs, they work on the souls of people and destroy them. That is why you should be more careful and more selective in your beliefs.

D: Are there ways to identify these people when we meet them?

MG: Determine if their ultimate goal is their belief in God, or in their belief in just themselves, in just glorifying themselves.

D: Is that not a weakness of all healers though? What we call a human frailty? Sometimes I hear people say, "Well the healing did not last very long", does this mean the healing was not necessarily good, or that these healers did not have the right source for their power?

MG: Yes, that is right.

D: Where is the responsibility of patients to change their lives. If they do the same things, surely they create the same problems again.

MG: That is why you tell them they should be more selective. That is why Jonah was emphatic in saying that you should be faithful to your mission. Do not let others influence you.

(1)   Nelson K. Edgar Cayce's Hidden History of Jesus. Virginia Beach, Virginia; 2000.
(2)   Fuller J. G. Arigo: Surgeon of the Rusty Knife. Frogmore, St Albans, Herts, England: Granada Publishing Ltd; 1977

(3)   Martin H. J. III. The Healing Ministry of Jesus Christ. Makati, Philippines: Loyal Printing; 1986

Donald McDowall

VALUE OF STATUES AND MANDALAS

D: I want to ask you something about the mandala on the wall next to this room. It has been creaking lately. Is something happening?

Master Gordon: You should be glad.

D: I thought the mandala was going to fall on me.

MG: You are becoming more sensitive. You are becoming a clairaudient.

D: So you mean other people cannot hear those noises.

MG: True.

D: The sound is like the metal creaking. That is what I hear.

MG: We are manifesting ourselves to you. These are tests. We are very happy you are passing these tests. We do things to make you understand and to make you more aware of your surroundings. We are very happy for that. You have passed another test.

D: Can you tell me what the significance of that mandala is? Is this something that you have guided the healer to have, or just an artefact of devotion?

MG: The mandala is just like the statues of the Catholics in their churches. This one goes back to the Amish.

D: The Amish? They are German people. How is that?

MG: Did you know that they put this stuff around them to prevent people from casting a hex. This is what they use. These are added to their works, embroideries and clothing.

D: I thought this one came from Egypt.

MG: This one, no. This is of German origin and was just a sign they used. We are talking of the hex sign, the eight dials or radials. Your friend added the triangle inside the mandala.

D: What do the hexagonal eight eyes represent?

MG: The eight winds, the southern winds.

D: Is there a way I should use the mandala more effectively?

MG: What you are doing now is right. The mandala really has no power, you are just using it to symbolise the power of the Divine. In itself the mandala is nothing, just as the Santo Ninó *[statue of the infant Jesus]* in your room is nothing, in itself.

Donald McDowall

HOW TO GET RID OF FEAR WITH PRAYER

Jonah: Join hands. Dear God, we know you are with us. Cast off this negative spirit from us. Surround us with your white light. Do not let fear enter our midst. We are doing our best to communicate with you, Father. Embrace us with your light. Embrace us with your love. I command you, evil spirit, get out of this house and stay out. You have no room in our hearts. Evil spirit of fear, you are not wanted here, we are casting you down to hell.

FEAR – THE ENEMY OF HAPPINESS

D: Why do the negative spirits visit us?

Jonah: You do not know how to harness your emotions. Remove fear from your heart, fear of being rejected, fear of trying something new. Like doing something good for others, like biting your tongue when you want to say something sarcastic. Do not be afraid. If you let fear rule your heart, you lose half your life. I do not mean you will die; I mean the happiness you will gain from doing something good is lost if you have fear. Do not be bitter. If someone strikes you, do not him back. Do not say, "He hit me first, so I have to hit him". Let that be his cross, you do not have to stoop to his level. Be a lady or a gentleman.

LIMITS OF THE HUMAN BODY AND DISCIPLINE

Jonah: In some ways, I am very pleased with your children, but I fear a few of them do not understand or do not listen.

D: We have made a lot of changes with them in a short period of time.

J: That is why I am happy. That is why I am well pleased. And that is true, even for your little girl.

D: Doing everything at once is hard. I think they will be influenced by their experience.

J: We do realise that their bodies limit human beings.

D: That must be frustrating for you.

J: Not really, because I have been there. What frustrates me is when they know what is right and wrong and still follow wrong.

D: This is the challenge of the human body. Is not the purpose of being here and getting a human body to learn discipline.

J: That is why we are teaching your children to discipline themselves.

HEADACHES AND OBEDIENCE

Jonah: We will discuss something about headaches.

D: What do you want to tell me about headaches?

J: Later on. There will be some scolding.

D: I have seen headaches occur. I have watched the healer when he is working. If he is not concentrating when doing his healing he gets a headache. Is this what you mean? Annie had a headache the other day and I kept asking her why she had this headache. She would not talk to me about the headaches.

J: That is why there will be some scolding. Prepare yourselves. I will not be there. Master Gordon will speak to you.

D: Is this on Wednesday?

J: No, tonight. Wednesday, I take over to talk to your children, and later Master Gordon will talk to them too. Tonight Master Gordon will talk to you about headaches.

D: I am looking forward to understanding more about headaches, but I do not want any.

J: Then obey, so you do not get headaches.

D: Thank you.

HEADACHES

Jonah: Headaches are physical manifestations of different things. Number one: if you have an empty stomach and you do a lot of work, you get headaches. I am not talking here of just physical work.

Number two: if you have a lot of things on your mind and you feel crowded, overwhelmed by this, you get headaches.

Number three: if your mind and your heart do not agree, you get headaches and stomach aches. What else?

D: Is this the same, as Master Gordon would have explained to us about headaches?

J: We are talking of physical things here, things that your children can easily understand, because some cannot understand deeper things. If you want to discuss headaches further, you can talk to us in private, or any one of you can ask in private.

DEVELOPMENT OF MEDITATION

Jonah: You have not mastered yet the art of concentrating, of meditating. You have just gained 85 percent. Try to do at least a 95 percent, and then we will help you go a rank higher. You are already high with your development and we are very proud of that. We like people who are committed to their mission. We appreciate people like you. That is why we help you with your children and your friends. These are benefits you get in return for the commitment.

D: Is there anything that I can do to improve my concentration.

J: Discipline. Discipline and focussing. We will review this. When you meditate remove everything else from your mind. Relax and let God work inside you. Make sure positive energy comes into your body when you open yourself. Pray. We will always be there. Envelop yourself in white light. These are just reviews, we know you already know this. And think only of God. God is your focus.

The next step is your books. After the books communicate with different people through letters, through seminars, through healing. These are the things you will be doing.

D: Yes, I do, thank you.

J: That is why completing your self-discipline, your focusing, is very important.

D: I understand.

POWER TO HEAL DIFFICULT PROBLEMS

D: I have another question. One of the patients Annie helped me with was having a lot of trouble with his back and his legs; they were becoming very painful. I asked her to look inside his body to see what the trouble was. I tried to help him. He is always very co-operative. I wanted to ask if he will be able to get better with what I do, or if I should send him to another doctor for surgery.

Jonah: You can only relieve pain at this stage. This has taken root between his bones. He needs medical assistance.

D: This problem seems much harder than others we have worked on.

J: A person confident he can do everything has no use for God. He has already defied the power of God over him. Your attitude is right. You get your power only from God. Just stay on the right course, we will provide the rest. Remember the story of Lucifer. He became too confident and defied God. That is why we have the Devil. Free will is to defy or conform to God's law.

D: Some people I see I know I can do nothing physically for, but after I prayed for them they got better. I am grateful for that.

J: The pureness of your intention is what we appreciate most in you. That is why we chose you. We know your main purpose is to help people.

D: I was concerned about this man.

J: Even if you do your best, or more than your best, if the body of the person concerned is not willing to heal itself, is not willing to co-operate, you can do just so much.

D: I have counselled him about that.

J: You have to. In all your healings, you have to counsel your patients.

D: I feel I am an example of the problems that my patients have. I feel the strength of my body feeds their fatigue.

J: That is why we are turning the table on you.

D: I get the message. I will try to strengthen myself for when he comes on Monday. If God gives me the opportunity, I will do my best to help him.

J: Zechariah will be there for you, call on him.

D: Yes, he always helps me; I know he is there to help me. I am sorry that I am weaker than what he would like.

J: This is because you spend too much energy and you do not save. Save some for yourself.

Donald McDowall

THERE ARE NO ACCIDENTS IN LIFE AND WHERE OUR PROBLEMS COME FROM

Jonah: The medium I am using now is physically sick. You have to bear with her body. That you gather tonight is rather important and I thank you.

I am about to tell you nothing earth shaking, but have been assigned to relate the messages of the father. Goodness and evil are everywhere. What you want to accept is up to you. Both sides will try to get inside your head and inside your heart. If you let fear rule your body and your mind, evil will start to gnaw inside you and consume you. Do not let this happen. Each of you has challenges and tests. Some of you might complain: "Why do I get this every day; why don't I get a holiday?" The answer is, you are being strengthened for something in the near future.

Don: Will you explain more to us Jonah?

J: Each of you has a mission in life. Nothing happens by accident. Your meeting together is no accident. The stranger talking to you now – and I mean the medium I am using now – did not come here by accident. Her purpose is to communicate with you and try to help you lighten up your problems. You cannot focus properly on your problems when they are too close to you.

Most problems are created by our emotions. We let fear rule us. Or we give fear room in our hearts. Once fear enters our heart, all that is negative starts to happen. If you do not give room to fear and have faith in the goodness of God, no matter what others do to us, fear will never touch us, will never touch our lives. Always bear that in mind.

WHY HEALERS RISE AND FALL

D: Tony Agpaoa, was a famous Filipino healer; do you know if he has reincarnated or is still a spirit? (1)

Master Gordon: He is still a spirit, but he will be coming in the later part of the 1990's. He has a lot to make up for. He had done a lot of good things, but drowned in his fame and power. Now he has to amend for that.

D: I have visited his house and prayed in his chapel. It has a special feeling.

MG: Presently his spirit is wandering, waiting for a suitable background and body, and circumstance.

Why are you interested in him?

D: I am interested in learning from his mistakes, so I will not repeat these. I believe learning from experience is better than making my own mistakes.

MG: That is true. At the start, he was pure; pure of intention, pure in his heart. Because of his poverty, his weakness for money came out and devoured him. Let that be a lesson to you.

D: Who was his spirit guide who worked with him?

MG: His guide was Chief White Feather.

D: Like Rama for the healer?

MG: Yes, but these are just names, a projection of the guides intentions and imagination.

D: Are they masters like you?

MG: No, but these people *[spirits]* learn fast, like a comet shooting up and coming down as fast.

D: I understand that when the healers would go to the caves and to the mountains and sacred places to pray, they find spirits to enter their bodies and give them power.

MG: You should be very careful. Not all spirits hovering are from the good.

D: Were these from the good?

MG: Which spirits are you referring to?

D: Rama and White Feather.

MG: Yes, because of the goodness coming out of their teachings. Weakness in the man overpowered the goodness in their hearts. You should always be cautious. Always check yourself. Do not get stuck on to your weakness. By this time, you know your weaknesses.

D: Is that why my development is slower in some respects than for some of these other people?

MG: Yes; because we want to polish you. Your mission is not just to heal the physical man. If you notice, these healers around you just heal the body, very shallow. The human being also needs healing in the spirit and the mind. A healer should never forget the unseen part of the man. Most of these healers just focus on what is obvious. You have passed that stage; the time is now to tune in to spiritual healing.

D: I try to do that.

MG: Just watch for those weaknesses, that is where the Devil will come in. Always arm yourself with the white light in everything that you do, in every moment of your life.

D: I try to do that.

MG: Do not tell me you try to do it. When you say you try, you still make room to do the opposite. I do not want you to give any room for negative forces.

D: I understand what you are saying, but sometimes the light does not always come as quickly as I ask. This is getting better, but is not yet instantaneous. Maybe you can help this to come more quickly.

MG: Clear your mind of all thoughts. Focus only on God. Learning to focus has always been your weak point when meditating.

D: I understand, but sometimes focussing is difficult when I have many responsibilities.

(1) Sherman H. "Wonder" Healers of the Philippines. Los Angeles, California: DeVorss & Co.; 1967.

Donald McDowall

ARIGO AND DR FRITZ – SPIRITS ARE ASSIGNED

D: I wanted to ask you about a healer called Arigo, who practiced in Brazil, at Sao Paulo. He was very famous and had a spirit guide called Dr Fritz[4]. This spirit guide had a great knowledge of medications and treatments and was able to help many, many people. I met a man from there who now lives here. He explained to me that even though Arigo died, the spirit guide came to another doctor and works with him. This other doctor practices as a gynaecologist in the daytime, and at night as a spiritual healer. Do spirits have access to knowledge they need to help a person, or are some spirits more specialised in healing and surgery.

Master Gordon: Just as Zechariah worked with you and Lucas first, and Paul had access to knowledge, book knowledge, and Jonah to give him instructions, so have these other spirits. This depends on the requirements of a person. We supply that. Jonah was a soldier. He was assigned to this person because he knows military discipline, philosophy, tactics, and can work better with him[5]. This is the same with your doctor and with you. Each spirit is assigned for a person's need.

(4)   Arigo: Surgeon of the Rusty Knife. John G. Fuller, Crowell Co, New York, 1974.
(5)   The Practice of the Presence of God, Conversations & Letters of Brother Lawrence. Oxford, England: Oneworld Publications; 1993

USING YOUR GIFTS AND LOSING THEM – TEAMWORK

D: Some people do not share their good fortune. Some healers do not share their gifts. People are selfish.

Master Gordon: The gift given you, will be taken away if not used properly. Or if not taken away, will not prosper. What use is a tree that cannot give shade or cannot bear fruit? The gift will wither, or people will not seek you.

D: I have trouble understanding this. In my work, the more I give, the more I receive. My business is always busy if I try my hardest to give as much as I am learning.

MG: This is a basic truth and works all the time. God does not give a gift to be put into a drawer or a box. He gives a gift to be used positively. A gift not used and just put into a box will get lost, 99 percent. Those wanting it will steal the giftb.

D: When some friends who are healers first came, I asked them if they would like to have assistants who were developing healers to help them. I was surprised that they did not want any help, because if those people helped they would have brought many other people to be helped also. Now I understand why.

MG: It hurts, does it not?

D: Yes. I cannot understand why it is like that. In the beginning they wanted so much to give, but now—

MG: Because – answer me, why?

D: I think because in some way they do not want to receive any more, they do not want to receive the publicity, they do not want to receive the hard work, they are tired.

MG: Why do you think people delve in privacy?

D: What do you mean?

MG: Their work, their field of work, deals with a lot of people, mingling with them, healing them, communicating with them. Then why is it that their work is kept in secret and not shared by a lot of people? Tell me – I am helping you understand. I am waiting for your response.

D: I think they do not – I think they give credit to God, I do not see a problem with that. But I think it is because they want it to be kept secret, they do not want other people to talk about it.

MG: Why?

D: Because they do not want the pain that goes with that.

MG: What pain are you talking about?

D: The more you talk about something, the more people want to know and then you get lots of reporters and then you get criticism and I think they have not worked through how to deal with being questioned by the public.

MG: Is that how you perceive this? There is more.

D: I think this reflects on their character. They have progressed so far, but do not want to go further.

MG: I will put this to you bluntly. A team needs at least two people. If only one person is working in a team, that person will get tired. If a person is being stopped from doing what he has to do, he will get tired and just sit down and let the other do the work. One of them is sincere, but cannot always struggle against the other person. They should be working together. He lets the other one rule. What the other wants may be totally different from what he has to do. One weakens, the other one gains strength. The weaker one loses trust in himself and loses power.

To make a team work well there must be a goal. That is the number one rule. You must pull together and believe in the same thing. You must support one another and each must have confidence to produce something positive to help the other, and not to destroy the other person, or to hinder that person from doing what he has to do. Learn from this, because you and your wife are a team, are one. This is why others are not productive.

D: I understand what you say.

MG: This is why I am teaching you to treat the gift you have kindly. Do not abuse the gift. Do not put the gift on a shelf. Both of you should nourish the gift so you reach out to many people. Both of you have the same belief. Work on that. Do not go against each other. I know that you are supporting each other. Always be one. You may have some emotional hiccups every now and then, but emotion is separate from what you are working on. Annie will not betray you. I know you will not betray her. You are a good team. Strengthen that team.

USING HEALING ENERGY

D: When I am doing my healing, I sometimes close my eyes. Sometimes I feel I should open my eyes and see what I see. When I am doing my healing, is it better looking at or beyond the physical?

Master Gordon: Decide on a case-to-case basis. At times concentrate your energy into that person, and at times be more with it, depending on how much a person needs.

D: Do they get more if I close my eyes, or more if I concentrate on the physical?

MG: When you open your eyes that person's need is not strong. Closing your eyes proves only your need to concentrate more in giving that person healing. The condition is more serious, and calling for more concentration. When you open your eyes, the energy exerted is not as strong as when you close your eyes. Be discriminating. Sometimes you give a person more energy than is needed, wasting the energy you exert.

D: I am trying hard to discriminate. This is difficult for me.

FATIGUE AND SPIRIT INVASION

D: You do not sound like Master Gordon.

Evil Spirit: How do you know?

D: Was Jesus born in the flesh?

ES: That is a lot of nonsense. There was no Jesus at all.

D: Well I think that you should leave so that Master Gordon can come.

ES: Why?

D: Because you are not him, and he has authority over us.

ES: And I have authority over this body now.

D: You should leave so that Master Gordon can come to speak with us.

I ask you to leave now so that he can come, and leave this body alone so that he can come.

ES: Not too fast. I want to use this body.

D: I command you to leave. I command you to leave now. You do not have permission to be in this body; you must leave.

Please God, give me strength to cast this spirit out so that your messenger will be able to speak with us.

Master Gordon are you there?

Master Gordon can you speak with us?

Master Gordon: I am here. Thank you very much.

D: I have prayed for Annie's protection, yet this spirit still came. Why is that?

MG: That is because her body was very tired. It is the same as when your body gets sick and tired. The body when tired weakens. The body when weakened can barely resist an onslaught by the evil one. That is why we always tell you to reserve some energy for yourselves so you do not weaken quickly.

THE VARIOUS POWERS OF HEALING

D: Talking with the healers, I am told they often get their power meditating for long periods. We are working physically while we are meditating. Is the process the same, only a different way? Or are we talking about two completely different ways of achieving the end.

Master Gordon: There are different ways, but the same result. As we have mentioned before, you will be dealing most with the spirit of man, and the body follows. Your results will show physically, but your approach is different.

D: What is the reason?

MG: Have you not learned from discussions with your patients? Healing starts from within a person. A doctor or a healer's power is limited unless a patient co-operates from the heart, and you have accessed that part of the patient. You have worked, and you are working on the spiritual side of man. You must have observed that when a doctor is limited on the physical level he has to work on his other faculties to progress faster. We are showing you the harder way of healing man. You must have had faster more positive results these days than before?

D: That is true.

MG: Common healers, usually work just on the body giving hope to people. They do not work on the root cause, which you are doing now. This is like cutting grass, not pulling out the roots. Grass will still grow if you do not pull out the roots. What you are doing is pulling out the roots to stop the grass re-growing.

D: Thank you.

THE PATH OF THE SPIRIT AFTER DEATH

Master Gordon: The spirit does not stay idle. Your guide has to grow spiritually as well, and that is what he is learning now. He has to practice that when he goes back into the earth. Just like yourselves. In the past when you died you went out of your body. Your spirit went out of your body. You reviewed the life you had, finding out where you went wrong, and how you abused your body and your spirit. You worked on your weaknesses spiritually. Now you are back to the physical form, you work on these things physically.

D: Is this what people call the judgement day?

MG: The judgement day, as you put it, will come at the very end of your mission, before we take you out of your body.

You will be asked how far have you progressed, or did you progress at all? Did you succeed in your mission by coming back? Or did you just potter around?

A DISCUSSION OF GIFTS

D: Can you make things materialise, Master Gordon. When I watch the psychic surgeon at work, I see him make pus or diseased tissue materialise outside the body. Are you able to do that?

Master Gordon: What he does is meant for non-believers and those with a frail belief in God, helping them strengthen faith in God and themselves. Somebody of your ranking has no purpose in materialising tissue.

D: I want to work better and do more of my mission. I am handicapped feeling like this.

MG: Explain what you mean by better.

D: I cannot talk properly, making concentration difficult and painful talking to people. I feel I am functioning only at about two-thirds of my energy.

MG: Why?

D: Because of this head. Because of this sinus.

MG: You have to learn again, give yourself time. That has always been so with you and Annie. You are like a ping-pong ball; if not on one side of the net, on the other side. You have to balance yourselves.

D: That is why I was asking if you could take the congestion from my head so I can get better.

MG: I will do that for you. I will do that through Annie. We will remove that thing blocking your passageway.

D: When will you do that?

67

MG: Tomorrow night. If you will give me time. Relax, meditate, and after that meditation we will do the healing for you.

D: If I have a patient who needs help like this, and while I am working with them, can I ask you to help me do the same with them?

MG: I cannot promise every time. That is not what we are supposed to work on. I am doing this to ease your pain. But in time we will do that, as you progress. We promised you this long before. We have to work on you first before we can work with other people through you.

D: Some people need help. They have arthritis, and serious problems needing help. This would be so much quicker for them. They would not have to suffer so much.

MG: You are asking for material manifestation, for physical manifestations of healing.

D: The body is physical. If physical injury is got rid of, then healing is much quicker.

MG: Always remember, the source of all maladies, the sources of illnesses is the spirit, or the mind of a person. We work on that to arrest pain. Is that not more important than manifesting all this physically?

D: Bringing all three parts of the triangle together is much better. I understand what you mean, but this is like writing a contract. Once you sign, the contract is complete. Physical manifestation is like the signature.

MG: Physical manifestation is going back to lower ranking. Do not you realise that? Have you not learned that yet?

D: I understand going back to lower ranking if the focus is just on the physical. If the physical weakness were preventing the person from having a more beneficial and spiritual life, then physical manifestation would seem to have a higher purpose.

MG: We will work on you first.

D: Am I in error?

MG: No, I am not going to argue with that. These are like using crutches when you can walk on your own.

D: Is not the physical body a crutch for his spirit? Is this not a restriction that we have to use?

MG: Giving us bodies, is an expression of God's love.

D: Then is not a further expression to be able to keep the bodies strong?

MG: You are driving us, and you are giving yourself responsibility for these people's maladies. People are responsible for their own bodies.

D: They come to us to learn how to become more responsible and to gain respect for what we say. They learn by what we share with them.

MG: There are two ways of looking at this. One is the positive way. We understand that. People who you work with might find this difficult to digest. We understand your motive. We will do this for you.

D: I worry a lot about these people; many are very good people, many are just learning. A little encouragement is needed. A carrot on a stick. They can see a bit further ahead. Some are like lambs; they need to follow a little more.

MG: There are people who might find you tampering with the forbidden, if you do this. Not everybody would understand. They might start to think, and I am here to protect your interest. Some might find this is from God, others might think it fakery and the rest might find you had a contract with the Devil himself.

D: Well, Master Gordon, my whole life has been in contradiction to most people. I was brought up in a family who did things differently. I grew up in a church that was alien to many churches. I went on a mission to follow God's will, when my friends would be in university and studying, and then I studied chiropractic, not main medicine, and I am considered a witch-doctor for that. To me, this is no different, only an extension of purpose in my life. If I can be of more help, then this is no different from the journey I have been on for this last 40 years. Does that seem unreasonable?

MG: No. We just wanted to make sure that you really are decided on this. We will help you with that.

D: I do as much as I can, but know there is more. I have seen more. I know people are able to understand what I say. Sometimes they need an extra push to commit themselves.

Maybe I ask too much. I do not mean to do that, but that is what my heart says. Is that unreasonable?

MG: We understand your point. Be ready for the consequences.

D: I do not take lightly what you say. I know you will help me.

One thing I would like to help most is Annie's lungs because I worry about that. I think there is a deep-seated infection needing to be cleaned out.

MG: She was exposed to chain-smokers. This is a little background of what she has undergone. When she came here to Australia was the first time she started to breathe freely. Work from there.

D: I realise that. That is why I wanted to be able to help her more. I can help, but to go back through all those years really needs the power – a miracle. Physical cleaning is needed. Do you understand?

MG: We will help you. But as you ask more, you have to give more.

D: What do you ask of me, that I have not given?

MG: You have to become more disciplined. As you progress, you should be stricter with yourself, discipline yourself. Discipline yourself in the sense that as you give more energy, generate more energy, you have to learn to budget properly. Excess baggage should be cut off. Discipline yourselves also with regards to worldly matters. Do you understand?

D: What do you specifically refer to?

MG: The temptations of the world. If you intend meditating, do not let your friends, even your family, divert you by their asking you to do this or that for them, or to go out with them. Learn to discipline yourself. The Bible says if your right eye makes you sin, remove it; if your left hand makes you sin, cut it off. Do you understand? That is, as we give you more, you have to give more as well.

D: Did not Jesus summarise that in loving God as you would love yourself?

MG: He had great discipline. He could have easily made money at the time, or could have taken advantage of the people who turned to him.

That is what we mean, that is what we are asking of you.

D: I understand Jesus was disciplined.

MG: You should not totally abandon the world. If we beckon, you have no choice. Do you understand?

D: Have I not followed everything you have asked so far?

71

MG: There will be more demands on you. As you care more, as you give more, generate more of your energy into healing these people, you will become more tired and you need more rest. You need to budget your time and effort more. That is what we mean.

If you plan to go out with friends, usually you do not look at the time. When you start looking at the time, you will have your curfew. We realise you do not touch alcohol, that is good. We also realise you do not touch cigarettes and other women. That is good. Maintain that. Your energy can be spent on other things. Anger is spent energy.

D: I discussed this today with Annie.

MG: You can expend that energy positively.

D: You know my heart, I do not anger easily. Do you see anger in there?

MG: There are rightful angers as well. Do not let anger eat inside you.

D: Have I not tried to overcome those?

MG: In some ways, yes, but still you let some people take advantage.

We will discuss this further Saturday, before we heal you, because we will have a long meditation. Do prepare yourself.

D: How would you like the meditation to proceed?

MG: In private, by yourselves. This is team work between your and your wife. As we have mentioned before, we will use her body to reach you.

D: While she heals my sinus, I can heal her lungs. Will that be permissible?

MG: We will do this gradually. You cannot expect miracles overnight.

D: I always hope for the best.

MG: And we are giving you the best.

Shall we shake hands on that?

D: I am a man of my word.

MG: This will be more demanding. As you learn, do not let go of your discipline. Is that understood?

D: I have always tried to do what God has asked me to do.

MG: We will do this step by step. We will show you first and then help you through discipline and work.

D: At one stage, Master Gordon, I was going to ask Annie to come and help me to do some of this, but I did not feel the time was right and that she would like to do that. Was I rejecting the promptings, or should I have carried through?

MG: Now is not the proper time. Before you can heal others, you have to be strong yourself. Your wife can heal. This has been proven many times, she just does not use it. Rather like buying a car and just putting it in a garage. She is waiting for you. We will work on that.

D: Thank you, I will look forward to that and prepare.

MG: Have faith in your mission and do not to be persuaded by others to go to walk with them on their journey. Jonah has discussed this before and I am going to discuss this again. Never be tempted to join other people's journeys to lighten their way. When you do that, you will lose yours. You will be. Others have already approached you to interest you in their different beliefs and practices. Let these words be a warning to you.

D: I remember I have been warned many times about this.

MG: Do not take this lightly. The pain Annie felt then was just a little reminder. She knew better not to experiment. Next time could be more serious. That is our discipline.

D: Did Jesus discipline as harshly as this?

MG: He went into the desert fasting for 40 days and 40 nights. Many people had rebuked him in his own community, and still he pursued this. He disciplined himself. Like a horse, he put blinkers so as not to see sideways, but focus on that in front of him. That is why he succeeded. Even as a man he lived a life of poverty, but of dignity as well. He was tempted in different ways, even temptations of the flesh, by many women, not just by one. Sure, he had his own woman, but as he went from town to town, there were other temptations.

D: Did he have children?

MG: Many believed he had, but he did not. He had many brothers and sisters, but he had no children of his own. He had a wife. His having a child would serve no purpose.

D: In the book "Mary's Message to the World", his family, with all the brothers and sisters, is described. Is this fairly accurate[6]?

MG: Not 100 percent accurate. Some embroidery is to be expected. We are asking you to properly supervise the writing of your second book so this will not be flavoured by the way others see it.

D: When I ask you for specifics, you make the comment about flavourings. I never get a specific answer from you; is there a purpose for that?

MG: In time, we will answer you in detail everything that you ask us. Presently we have to work on your perception. You still have, at times, a tendency to take us literally in everything. There are messages that we send you, physical messages that we send you that sometimes you overlook.

One day last week we tried to tell you something through a little girl who came to visit you. You did not see this. You did not see. You did not have a projection. We were trying to tell you to give her a message. She waited, but nothing happened.

The other night you went to a place, a foreign place, and there was an old woman. You touched her; you talked with her, but did not see us there. You did not recognise us. Why do you think she stayed there so late? She left and she returned, because she was waiting for you. I was waiting for you.

D: We talked with her and listened to her.

MG: You did not recognise did you?

D: She told us about her life and her story.

MG: She wanted to be touched.

There are little things; unexpected, that bear messages. Look closely. The little woman who met you also needed help.

D: We stayed to talk with them. I tried to do my best for them.

MG: This was a call for help, not just from these old people, but also for themselves.

D: I recognise that. We tried to address that too.

MG: These are lonely people, needing to be cared for as well.

D: I was happy to be there and to do what I could to help them. And Annie was very – I think that she impressed them as well.

MG: When you walk, do not overlook the flowers; even the flowers of the weeds have their own beauty. Recognise that. Acknowledge that. These people need to be cared for. Not only the roses or the orchids need be addressed. God takes care of everybody and of everything. Work on that.

(6)   Kirkwood A. Mary's Message of Hope. Nevada City, CA: Blue Dolphin Publishing Inc; 1995

A DISCUSSION OF GIFTS, NO. 2

D: We have worked hard to do the things you have asked, and I know that you have our best interests at heart. Today we discussed this issue. I hope Annie understands what we were discussing, that if our bodies are stronger, our work is made easier.

Master Gordon: We did not understand what she was doing. She asked why did you have to do certain things to get the wishes you are asking for. Tonight you asked us to heal your sinusitis and her lungs. She understands that. But what she cannot understand is when healing all this, why do we have to impose so much on both of you. Why cannot you just have this free, to further the success of the mission.

D: Does she have enough credits to be able to influence you?

MG: I know in her heart that if she says she will do something, she will, in a roundabout way.

D: Am I unfair? Am I pushing too much?

MG: You are asking added loads at a time when you are very vulnerable. When you ask for things, you should first see how much you could carry. Do not add, five more pounds to the weight you are carrying now, when you know that you can carry an extra two pounds. In time, as we have promised before, as we have discussed before, we will grant you all these wishes, all these things that you need in your work, in your mission.

D: I do not want to distress her, Master Gordon; if she does not feel comfortable with this, then I would prefer that extra conditions not be added.

MG: We will do this gradually. What you are asking is an abrupt change from what you are now. We are not discussing your body, but what you requested, that you learn how to heal the physical body.

We will do that, we will teach you step by step how to do things, in keeping with what you can take.

D: I appreciate that. However, I know Annie would like us to move forward as quickly as we can.

Do you feel comfortable that we can handle more? Or are you keeping a little in reserve so that we stay ahead of ourselves?

MG: I would like to do this at a slower pace, because I do not want you to fail. The pressure might be too great. You have reached so far; you have done so much not to fail now. That is what we are trying to say to you. This is the same with Annie.

We understand the limitation of the human body. That is why we want to do this in a certain time. You have been complaining about the pressure that you are having with Annie's work. If we impose more discipline, added discipline on you, this really would be taxing.

Do you remember during one of your friend's lectures, he had to undergo rigid disciplining at a particular time? His discipline, or initiation, was limited because of his body's capacity.

You are asking for more. We do not want the body to crack with that pressure, like putting a hot pot into a freezer. We work gradually; that way everybody wins. You get what you want and complete the mission. In that way we get what we want from you.

D: Did you reach an agreement with Annie yet?

MG: No, not yet. But I think she understands now. As you said, she really is a bargain hunter.

D: Can you make some concessions for her?

MG: Yes.

D: I would rather that she had the healing. Her health is a priority. I can carry my own pain without great difficulty, but for her, there is more of a struggle. I know she does not complain. I would like it if there was something you could do for her.

MG: That is a sign of a true healer; unselfish and caring. I am very pleased. She said the same thing to me: if need be, I give the healing to you since you are the one who is more exposed to people and the one that people go there to see. She said that she could get healing later, since she is in the background. Now I am very pleased.

D: I have given much to her and have no regrets. I want only the path we have begun to continue. I am happy with everything that we have done, and that our problems have become less. I want to be able to help Annie because this particular injury inside her body is serious. Her lungs are so important. Much better that she gets the healing.

So be it; whatever your will.

MG: We will grant both. We see the unselfish love you bear for one another. That is a very good sign of leadership, a one-ness in purpose. You have done very well, and I am very, very pleased.

I should share this with Jonah and the rest of the guides.

D: How many guides are responsible to you, Master Gordon?

MG: Those who have worked with you before, I am referring to them; because they have helped mould what you are now, what both of you are now, to each other.

D: We have chosen to rest tonight so that we could have this time with you.

MG: That is a very good decision. Even in the physical, you think alike.

Donald McDowall

STRENGTHENING YOUR BODY AND SPIRIT

Master Gordon: If you make room for Satan, even an inch, then he will use that to make a wedge in your faith in God. You are gathered here tonight, not to listen to my words, but to listen to your conscience. You can start from there. Examine your consciences and work on the weaknesses of your bodies and your spirits. If you entertain your weaknesses, you will be lost. If you recognise your weaknesses and work to eliminate them and strengthen yourselves, you will win the battle over the evil one.

If you find this hard, list down the things you have accomplished so far and the things you have failed to do, and make a balance. You can start from there. You do not have to verbalise it, but do this within yourselves.

At this stage of your lives, we cannot tolerate any more weaknesses. Thank you for acknowledging God, and thank you for trusting in Him and for welcoming this guide in your midst.

You are right to acknowledge that the responsibility you have brought on to your selves is great, but this is greater than you can imagine now. In doing this, you bring a light to the darkened hearts of men. Let that serve as a beacon to you, like a lighthouse in a storm.

GETTING RID OF NEGATIVE SPIRITS

Master Gordon: I COMMAND YOU, LEAVE THIS PLACE!

D: Is the Angel of Death coming again?

MG: YES. I AM IN CONTROL HERE. YOU HAVE NO ROOM HERE. LEAVE NOW OR IT WILL BE YOUR SWORD AGAINST MINE.

D: Thank you for your protection, Master Gordon.

MG: You forgot something again during your prayer. What if somebody else came instead of me?

D: I prayed for protection while the prayers were being said.

MG: When you pray for protection SAY IT LOUD.

D: Is it not enough saying it silently?

MG: We have discussed this before; spirits do not hear your thoughts. They react to what you speak.

D: I misunderstood that before.

MG: Always claim and affirm the protection of God.

D: We will do that from now on. Has he gone?

MG: Yes; he has me to contend with, not you.

D: Thank you for your protection.

HOW FOOD IS USED

D: We are using vitamins to help. We are paying attention to nutrition and the food is good. Annie will keep getting stronger.

Master Gordon: The strength comes from inside and the body reacts. The body will not bear good food the mind will not accept. Work with her body and with her energy. We work in her mind. You also work in that mind by just being there and being supportive.

CONFRONTING WEAKNESSES

D: How do we strengthen our weaknesses?

Master Gordon: A person cannot always stay where they are. You cannot run around in a circle and exhaust yourself with nothing. If one runs, one should run forward, and I am not saying one should run away, that is different. Often people run away because they feel hurt, but what they do not realise is that hurt goes with them, and festers. So one should confront and remedy that hurt. Build a better person to move on, and that goes for everybody.

Donald McDowall

CIRCLES AND HEALING

D: When we are doing the healing together with Solomon, I wanted to ask how that actually happens. If you just go to the person by yourself and help them, or is it when I put my hands on them and you work through me? How does the healing actually take place? Is the healing more effective if you do this by yourself? Is healing more effective working through a physical medium? At what stage does God intervene directly? Can you help me understand that?

Master Gordon: One at a time.

When I use a person, as I am using Annie now, she is not conscious and I can work freely. If I wanted to heal you now, I could do so easily quicker and better. If I want to use a human to heal the way we help you heal people, I use you and your sources of energy, tapping and using that energy. I direct you, show you what to do, like teaching a child how to hold a pencil and write. I hold your hand and direct you. That is the way. When you are fully conscious. There will be times when I would let you fall asleep and let me handle the person, completely. You and your energy would recede and let mine take over.

God comes in at anytime. He asks for your faith in Him. He can come at any time, even now, during our discussion, He can come to take your wife away, or heal her. Important here is the affirmation of your faith and trust in God, declaring to the world that you do trust Him. Confirming your commitment to Him in front of the evil ones.

Remember, all these actions, all these steps have their effect on the surroundings. There are times when people say, "I trusted in Him, but still He did not cure my wife". If the wife was not willing to continue with her life, or else – let us discuss your friend, a friend of yours who died. She did everything she could to extend her life, and still she died. When a person gives up hope that is when you lose your life. Even a spiritual life, when you lose hope, when a person says, "It is

84

useless; no matter how I try, I will always be bad", then you are confirming that you are bad.

How strong is your faith? There are those who completely trust in God and still die. What about them? Their mission is done, so they have to leave.

Going back to your question; how do I work with a person? As I said before, I can either direct a person on how to heal with you. You have confirmed your faith and trust in God; I use that and the energy as exerted to help you heal others. Now when your wife says to give more. I am just there directing how to process the energy inside your body.

If I am required, or I know that I have to do this myself, I can. I would ask permission from you. If you would let me, then I would take charge, with you half conscious.

I can do healing myself without using a human body; then why do I use a human body to heal? To let you feel God's power, to let you feel the spirit's energy and power to heal.

Why am I using Annie to communicate with you? I work better this way and **you** work better this way. As you have noted, you have a gift, but do not have the gift of seeing and perceiving the way she does, which is correct. Each one should acknowledge the gifts given him or her. Your wife acknowledges the gifts you have. She does not want to go into healing, because she says there is already one available. She did not have to come in and just concentrate on her other gifts, which work better. This is not competition, but help, support to one another. That way we work quicker and stronger. The same as your guide does not compete with me, or I with him. We work for one purpose alone, together, supportive of one another, that way we work as one. Just as the feet do not compete with the hands; or the left eye with the right eye. Do you understand now?

D: Yes, I understand what you are saying. We apply that to how the body works. Do you need a knowledge of the intricacies of the physical body to do your work better, do you just use my knowledge, or do you just apply the energy and go where it is needed?

MG: Everything works together. I tap into your knowledge of the human body, so you can better explain to the person involved.

D: Sometimes I go automatically to a part of a body before I think. If a problem recurs then something else comes into my mind. I can rationalise, do that and then think, which is usually the choice that I make. Sometimes I notice I can just go on automatic and not know what I am doing until finished.

I think, because I was not totally focussed on conscious control of everything I was doing, was the person really getting better as quickly as they could have, or was I being more obedient to the control of the spirit. I wonder if I have really done my best when I am not as conscious of what I am doing.

MG: The way you handle a child is different from the way you handle an adult man or an adult woman. We are discussing their character here. There are those who take life very seriously, like your wife, and there are those who put in a pinch of humour. There are those who do not want to face life. You tap into your knowledge of man as to how to handle these people.

Now with regards to their sicknesses, there are those times when you manage consciously and there are times when you give way to the spirit, to work on those people using your body.

HOW FEAR ATTRACTS EVIL

D: Yesterday I was walking down the hallway, out of my room, past a friend, and had a feeling like a butterfly inside my ear. There was a flicking noise on my ear, very loud, very conscious and uncomfortable. I asked Annie to see if she could feel anything. By that time the noise had gone. Do you know what that was?

Master Gordon: Do you not realise the evil one can work around you as well.

The fears you discuss with people, especially if you welcome those fears, they are used to bring fear around the Clinic. If you continued with a question in your heart, then the evil one would have used that as a tool to create more questions. When you took your wife with you, she was strong and did not fear, so the fear was easily erased.

Your friend's mother died but he claims she still follows him wherever he goes. He is suggesting that the mother is haunting him in the places he goes. Now with that suggestion, the evil one can work, because there already is fear and acknowledgment of that fear.

Donald McDowall

ABSENT HEALING – DOES IT WORK?

D: Is absent healing what Solomon does when he sends energy while he is with Annie? So I am an actual recipient of that, even though we are in different places.

Master Gordon: This is helping you help others. You said you do not often hear my sound when you do your healing. I gave you the reason for this. To work to maximum effect, remove the stress, then you will feel energy flowing inside you, strongly.

RESULTS OF MEDITATION

D: Does my preparing for meditation make a difference to how quickly the gifts will come?

Is it true the more I meditate and the more I prepare myself, the quicker that will be?

Master Gordon: This is beyond my reach, but is inside you. We can show you only bits and pieces. Once the circle is complete, you are on your way.

D: What do you mean, "the circle is complete"?

MG: Your thinking process, the way you process your thoughts, the way you accept what I tell you. The more you absorb, the faster you understand.

D: I see a light coming into my mind now. A light going on and off with the brightness altering – and becoming stronger.

MG: Is the light physical? Describe more fully what you see.

D: The light starts from the right and goes towards my left. My eyes are closed. The light pulses.

MG: How does seeing that light make you feel?

D: Warm. The light feels warm.

MG: Are you attracted to the light, or is the light attracted to you?

D: I am comfortable with that. The pulsing has stopped now.

MG: Is the light still there? Is it coming nearer?

D: Yes, the focus is more on the right, but has spread across.

MG: Touch the light.

Touch and feel, feel the texture, feel the warmth or coldness. Fix the light in your mind. You will be able to do this. Put the light wherever you want. You can place the light right in front of you, near your foot, or near your heart. Do it. Hide the light in your pocket and feel it sway. Feel the light sway; go up and down in your pocket, bounce. Or put the light in your mind again. Light up inside your head. You can control the light, or the light can control you. These are exercises. You wanted to see what Annie sees. We are giving you exercises to do this.

D: I understand.

MG: Describe the light.

D: Like the beam of a flashlight. Looking into the beam, I could see a face. I like having the light there. In some ways the feeling was like the experience I had when God came to visit.

MG: You will see this light from time to time, and exercise your mind until you develop fully and complete the circle.

HEALING – THE GRADES OF HEALING

D: I have noticed, Master Gordon, when I do my healing sometimes I feel a mass under my hand, inside the body, like a lump. I thought this was part of the person's body that I was feeling, and wondered if I am feeling the negative energy coming out and concentrating in one spot. Is it enough for this to form and dissipate?

Master Gordon: You can command the negative energy to leave the body. You have that power.

D: Will this manifest physically yet, or is this an invisible experience.

MG: You can feel because this is no longer invisible. If you want to work the way your friends work, this will happen later. Your guide will be the one to show you how to do this; he will be doing all this. These are beneath you. He will start with that and progress to a much higher form of healing.

D: When my friends say they have progressed from the surgery to a higher form of healing, is this what they mean?

MG: These physical manipulations are done only for people needing something tangible to hold on to, to believe in. A child learning to walk usually holds on to something to stand up. Usually they are propped up by the parents or by someone older than himself or herself until they feel more confident, learn to let go and walk erect.

These are given to some people to help others visualise the negativities in their bodies and rid themselves of those negativities. Those on a higher ranking, do not need this.

D: Is saying be gone enough?

MG: It is. Just as Moses did not have to physically prove everything.

D: How does that relate then to my work as a chiropractor, because that is very physical?

MG: That is your profession. These are physical ailments of people. Different illnesses or diseases are manifestations of spiritual suffering.

Chiropractic is concerned with physical needs; bad posture, accidents, injuries.

You help a child who has fallen down the stairs. You physically help because the child does not feel comfortable with a sprained ankle. This is physical.

A grown man who comes crying to you does not have a physical condition. There is something deeper. You inject your knowledge of the spirit to encourage him to move forward and to look up to God for help. They do not conflict.

D: I was wondering how these inter-related. This you have explained.

MG: Not all your patients come to seek spiritual guidance. Some need you only for their physical well-being, some kind of a balancing. Just give them what they ask for.

You have to practice speaking before people more. The time is coming when you need to speak to people of different nations about God and how He helps man heal himself. You will have many encounters, the man you were referring to is just one of them.

There is no co-ordination between his knowledge of the physical and of the spiritual. There is a conflict inside him, manifesting into his body. That is why he is undergoing this confining, or restricting disease.
We have discussed many times before that the physical body manifests only what is in the mind and in the heart.

WHEN NOT TO HEAL

D: Michael *[a patient]* was at the healer's clinic the other day when I was healing. I was helping the other people. I was not instructed to touch him. I was going to ask you why.

Master Gordon: He will drain your energy. The healer will be enough for him.

D: Is that why you asked me not to touch him? He has a good heart. I am not afraid of him.

MG: His needs are more than you can give at this time. You have to conserve energy. We do not mean that you should not share with others, but others' needs are minimal to his. His needs will deplete you of your reserves.

D: I have been tired and having headaches during the day. I could not understand, we were resting in the afternoon and yet I was having headaches.

MG: The same with your wife. You have to still build up that energy.

D: Why do some people have to work hard to build up energy, and for others, the healing is almost miraculous.

MG: Those whose healing is miraculous, have been prepared spiritually and mentally. Those who take time, have doubts, many doubts, holes in their minds' eye, holes in their spiritual lives needing to be patched up before healing takes place. There are those, whose belief, whose faith in God is complete, but the body cannot cope with healing any more. They have approached the healer too late. Their healing is just spiritual repair.

93

SPIRITUAL GIFTS

D: I was going to ask you about some people who have different gifts. In England there is a lady called Rosemary Brown whose gift is that music comes to her and she writes this down, even though she has no understanding of music[7]. Many famous composers give her information.

In Brazil, Louis Gasparetti was not an artist, yet when he mediated he could paint the Great Masters, with his feet, in the dark. I have seen that on video[8].

Do the guides do this, or is this simply an opportunity for the wandering spirits who have skills and who are waiting to come to the earth? Is this the same for some of the healers? Arigo said that a famous doctor used his body to give prescriptions to people and to do surgery with a rusty knife. I am trying to compare our experience with you and these experiences with those of other people. Seemingly there are different helpers. Is my logic describing this, or am I confused?

Master Gordon: You are not confused. What you have just said is right. Let me go further. Wandering spirits inhabits these people. Spirits with no specific bodies assigned to them.

D: So they are doing God's work by helping?

MG: That is why I am going to go further.

Always remember the Devil can duplicate what God can do, but with different motivation or different purpose. Now with these people, what is their purpose? Is it to glorify God or confuse man that the spirits of the dead have come back to life and confused history. Or is this to show man the wonders of God. You should find out for yourself, and for your own satisfaction, the motive behind all this.

D: I have met one of these. His name was Mathew Manning[9]. When he was a child he had psychic experiences, and an artist worked through him. He said God helped him help people. His responsibility is not as an artist any more, but as a healer. Now he dedicates his life to healing and helping people. His work was to show God had ways of working that are different.

MG: Clearly that power comes from where that spirit comes from. At times you will meet so-called healers who do not mention God. They say: "I did this. I will do these things for you." Which is different. There will be those that you will meet – ask your wife, she has met some – who would even offer to do for you that which is not according to the law of God, to love everybody.

To experiment with the unknown, to bring back the dead to life, what purpose will that serve; to experiment with sorcery, what purpose will that serve?

To heal people is different. Healing is a ray of hope in someone's life for God to work on. This is totally different from bringing a dead body back to life. This was different with God. He did this to show how powerful He was, how limitless He was. Tomorrow is Easter when God's triumph over death is celebrated. That man should do this does not follow. This proves nothing is hopeless if you hold on to God. The body will die, but the spirit lives and will not be condemned to hell. What the other party is doing is to bring back life, to give back life to dead bodies. For what purpose? He will attract these people and to make them do his bidding. This is contrary to God's law. You should not just look at the small frame, but project it. For what purpose is this person doing this or that? What you are doing is right.

D: Does this mean that you may also recruit those spirits waiting to come back to a new body to help for a particular purpose? Do you have all the knowledge needed, or do you use those spirits to assist?

MG: We use all the help we can. Sometimes, we even use the Devil. Even God made use of him many times over. Jesus, the man, was meditating when the Devil offered him worldly powers to worship him. This proved to man that even this favourite son was not free from temptation, but could overcome temptation.

How would you feel, or how would you think if a mere man was tempted with all the wealth in the world to worship the Devil. So we make use of even the Devil's help. If Jesus succumbed to the Devil, then the Devil has won over man. This man proved very strong in his faith in God. At the time, his energy was so low, perfect for him to be tempted.

You had your temptations, your chances and you proved yourself worthy of God's name. That is why we still work with you. If you had proved otherwise, we would have left you a long time ago. We encourage people who believe firmly in God. We leave them if they have made a different choice.

D: I noticed yesterday, when we were in the chapel at Tony Agpaoa's home *[in Baguio, Philippines]*, that when our friend Michael was with me and I closed my eyes, I could see the energy of the patient[10]. There was a dark part on the right side of his head and face. I could see that when my eyes were closed.

MG: Do you want me to explain, or are you just making an observation?

D: Seeing those parts of the body that are dark was a new experience for me. Does this mean I have to be in trance to experience that?

MG: Let us put this in perspective. You were not in full trance. You had always wanted to see what your wife sees. We gave you the chance. This man's mind is still wavering between the light and the dark. He has not made up his mind which route to take. He understands the concept, but he has not yet internalised it. Ask him if he believes in God. Ask him the difference between God and the dark forces. Test him the way you test the spirits that come inside this body.

D: I asked him if he believed in God; he said he did. We will have a conversation about which God.

MG: There are those who believe in the god of money, the god of the spirits, or the gods of bottled spirits, like the people downstairs *[we were in a room on the 2nd floor of a Motel. The bar was underneath our room.]*. They have different gods. They might even question you: "Which god do you believe in? The god of the healer, or in the Supreme One?"

D: Are you saying the healer is confused?

MG: No. What I am saying is, these people might question you.

They see things differently. You see things in a different light. As long as you believe in the right God, what they think does not matter. You will be meeting a lot of people of this persuasion, material persuasion. These will be the kind of people who need to be directed through example. If they see that you are happy with the kind of life that you live, they will be curious and start questioning, not you directly, but people around you until they get the courage, or until they are prepared to question you themselves. Your action, your behaviour, your physical being should reflect what is inside you. This is very important.

You are gathering all you will need on your journey. As we have mentioned before, many times, you will be going to places you never dreamed of going to. You will need all these skills.

(7)   Parrallel. Strange Talents. Music from beyond the grave, Page 24-27. Orbis Publishing, 1995

(8)   Manning M. The Strangers. Vale, Guernsey, C. I.: The Guernsey Press Company Ltd; 1995

(9)   [VIDEO] Savalas T. Channeling Voices from Beyond. Distributed by Eagle Entertainment Australia & New Zealand; 1991.

Donald McDowall

(10) Valentine T. Psychic Surgery. New York, New York: Pocket
      Book; 1975

NATURAL HEALING ENERGY

D: I have a photograph of the healer I want to ask about. You can see two lines of energy in the photograph that do not appear to be a spirit, as such. What do you think this is?

Master Gordon: Who is this lady?

D: She was a friend who had breast cancer. You can actually see the circular swirls with a line of white light in the centre of each swirl.

MG: Who took this picture?

D: One of the doctors in my group. She is quite sensitive.

MG: This is just electric energy emitted by the people around; good energy, not spiritual energy, but human energy. You have a name for this; aura. This is just physical energy of the people around all with being healed in mind. They come together and emit one aura. Good energy.

D: Does this mean that person is quite sensitive and can create energy.

MG: Yes. Each one of you has the ability to heal another person. If you use that properly, you get a positive result. A touch, a hello, a hug. You get that energy. A natural healing energy emitted by people.

D: Why does this not always show on film?

MG: A healthy body, can emit more positive energy than negative energy, so this is a healing gift. If the body is sick, or problematic, a negative force, negative energy is shown. Positive one, negative five is negative four. Negative two and positive five is positive three. The positive and the negative balance.

D: Will a patient take our energy as much if we are being protected?

MG: When you disarm yourself the patient attracts your positive energy. Your guard is down and he attracts the positive energy you have towards his negative energy. After a day is over, or after a meeting is over, you get tired. The patient gets that positive energy without knowing, without your even being aware until later. You should give only so much, do not let him take everything. He will learn to take just so much, and not take all. If you drain yourself two people will be sick instead of just one. A starving person who has been out in the sun for many days is fed little by little until the body can tolerate proper feeding. You start with drops of water, and then progress to juice and maybe a bite of bread. You do not throw him a whole chicken, his body would cramp and his condition would worsen.

The same with this man. He has been starved of positive energy, so he steals, unconsciously, and you suffer.

We have said before that you reserve some energy for yourself. If you do not you will not be able to talk with people. You will not be able to help others. You will be the one needing help.

D: I did not notice this type of weakness as much before I worked with so many people. Is this going to be the same when I go back to my work? Will I be more sensitive and able to do less?

MG: You will not be able to do less. You will be better able to discipline yourself. You will be able to help more people. Unlike before when you gave everything and left nothing, this is disciplining you to spread, give more to many other people, and reserve something for yourself. This is budgeting. You are very good at budgeting money. You are not very good at budgeting your energy. This time you have to learn.

HOW MIRACLES OCCUR

D: I was working on all the transcripts of our conversations last night. How did you make my tape recorder play music?

Master Gordon: I cannot explain. This is just the power of the mind. When you hear a humming sound you know I am making my presence felt by those around you. I cannot explain. I cannot explain how I can manifest myself in pictures. These are mysteries that are accepted. Even with you, surely you know when your wife is around, even without opening your eyes, even if she is not making any noise. You cannot explain. You know. There is that I can do this and am unable to explain how. Accept this.

D: I am glad I was sensitive enough to get the message.

Donald McDowall

SPIRITUAL CONSEQUENCES OF ACCIDENTS AND TRANSPLANTS

D: When we were travelling from Baguio one day we saw a young woman who had been killed. Her body was lying at the side of the road. This was very sad. When a person is killed, what happens to their spirit? I had the feeling I should pray for her spirit, that God would help.

Master Gordon: When things like this happen, the spirit becomes a wandering spirit. You have witnessed wandering spirits trying to get back into a body before. This was not planned by God, but by other forces.

D: We prayed for her, and I think her family would pray too.

MG: If people care for one another, they will pray hard for others.

D: Does this help the wandering spirit?

MG: No. The spirit still needs to come back and finish what has been started. That is why wandering spirits keep looking for a body, for a host, to finish their mission.

D: Does this have to be a newborn, or can these enter someone who does not have control of his or her body?

MG: You always have to be on guard. If you are not always thinking positively, and you let your minds wander, evil forces would use that to inject something foreign inside your head and you start thinking differently.

ST PAUL AND THE REASON FOR ILLNESS

Master Gordon: St Paul was blinded for a while and could not find his way.

D: Did that really happen?

MG: People get sicknesses to help them strengthen their spirit. Elizabeth's husband [John the Baptist's father] became dumb to help him grow spiritually.

You had to undergo physical pain, spiritual doubt, in your life to strengthen your character. Your wife had to undergo physical abuse to strengthen her faith. This is a challenge for her.

How you react, how you respond is important. Will you fight? Will you just wallow?

Some people are comfortable with their weaknesses. If there is a little change, they feel uncomfortable. You have to have the Third Eye *[spiritual awareness]* to feel how they respond to what you say to them. Your wife has that gift. She has her weaknesses. She is still struggling with her emotions, but I will never doubt her. The gift was given her when she was born. Her father and mother made use of that gift. They never doubted. Even professional people used her gift. She will not begrudge your using this to help in your profession.

HEALING PAIN – DO NOT RATIONALISE

Master Gordon: This is like having a quarrel with your wife when she is in pain. She tells you her pain, but you avoid the issue and make excuses. You should not make excuses for the pain. You should heal the pain. When your patient comes to your clinic and says I feel this, I feel that. You do not just say that is because you have been doing this, you have been doing that. You heal the patient.

BUILDING ENERGY

D: My friend trusted me. Some of my friends do not bother me. Only once in a while when they need a little help do they call me.

Master Gordon: You will be able to help more people if you reserve some energy. Do not spread yourself too thin, or you will not be able to give more. Share that with your friends. When you are starting to feel tired, stop for a little while, meditate for two or three minutes, and then go back to your patients. Relax a little.

WHY SOME HEALINGS DO NOT RESPOND

D: Are people who do not respond to healings tied up with the dark forces?

Master Gordon: Sometimes that is correct. Sometimes this is their time to leave. In other circumstances, they have not completely accepted God's power to heal and their bodies do not respond.

There are some dramatic healing and cures. The person concerned has accepted, without doubt, God's gift of healing. They have accepted spiritually, not just physically. You have heard of overnight healings. Your wife has done such healing and that was proved medically. She has that gift, but she does not want to use that.

DO NOT GET INVOLVED WITH OTHER PEOPLE'S EMOTIONS

Master Gordon: We are here to encourage you to become closer as soul mates, as husband and wife.

A word of caution though, do not get involved in other people's emotions unless you are invited. Even then, you should give only encouragement for them to feel better and think better. Do not let them depend completely on you. Do not play cupid. Get out of the way before people run you down. You cannot be the director or you will become a security blanket for others. In the end you might even be blamed for how they feel. Let them be responsible for their actions and decisions.

HELPING OTHERS

D: Have we been able to help those people coming to visit us as much as possible? Is there anything we have missed?

Master Gordon: A word of caution. And I am going to repeat this again and again until you learn by yourself. Do not be offended. Do not involve your emotions in dealing with these people. Do not involve yourself personally or you will be shackled to the problem forever. There are times when people seek an emotional excuse to rid themselves of a problem, and make other people be responsible.

D: We see that very often.

MG: There are those who want a problem out of their system so they see more clearly. You can help these people. All they needed was an expression of that deeply embedded in their heart and mind. Speaking out what is troubling them is a step towards resolving a problem. Be careful of those who do not want to take responsibility for solving their problems.

THE LIGHT OF GOD

Master Gordon: I will leave now. I would like you to meditate on your own, together, for a few more minutes. Let God flow into your beings.

D: I can feel the warmth and the light around us.

MG: Let that serve as your protection, your daily protection. That alone scares the evil one and stops him from touching you.

D: He has tried many times to influence us.

MG: He will not stop. Until the very end, remember that. Always arm yourself with the light of God.

ENERGY, HUNGER AND FASTING

Master Gordon: You skipped something. Remember hunger weakens the body.

D: We did not eat or have breakfast.

MG: You cannot go out in the world with a weak body. I understand now why Annie weakened so much.

D: So, we have to have breakfast before we go?

MG: You did not have dinner, as you mentioned, you did not have breakfast the following day, and then you went out to the healing. You spent some more energy there and she gave you back some of hers. Now I understand perfectly why she is weak. Do not neglect the body. The body is your tool. It is your means to help others. If as you mentioned, you prefer to sleep and do not feel very hungry in the evening, it is all right to sleep.

D: We will make sure that we eat meals. I thought that fasting strengthened energy. I did not realise fasting created such a weakness.

MG: Fasting is good, but you were working.

D: Do fasting and working not go together?

MG: Those who are fasting are usually meditating. Clearing the mind is fine, but they do not work physically. In your case, you fasted and you worked. You stopped taking food; at the same time you spent energy. These do not go well together. When you mix with a group of sick people your body weakens. You may not realise that when you spend energy with these people. Annie gives you back some of the energy that you lose.

FOCUS ON YOUR PARTNER

Master Gordon: Do not neglect your partner.

D: I will stay with Annie and help her. I should have been more sensitive and careful.

MG: Her way of supporting you is by giving you back some of the energy you spent with these people. Both of you should be aware and not neglect yourselves. Teach these people not to neglect themselves and their bodies.

D: Thank you.

HEALING PRIORITIES

Master Gordon: You wonder why we do not allow you to receive healing or even use the treatment tables these people use. You wonder why we let your friend use healing and not you.

D: The healings have helped me many times. Now I am a little confused because I encourage my friends and patients to come.

MG: There is no confusion. You are a doctor and feel their pains. You do not have to take the medication they take. The same here; we have already sanctified your bodies. The rooms are full of negativities coming from these sick people.

D: The healer is casting out those spirits. Are they not he and his wife helping these people by getting rid of those spirits?

MG: They get rid of those spirits from the bodies, but spirits do not disappear. They have neglected that. They should pray that these negative things leave them, forever. Their rooms have been taking in lots of negative energies, taken from ailing bodies. You are close to us; you are very, very, desirable to these negative ones. You feel more comfortable if you put on clean clothes rather than dirty clothes. So do these spirits. That is how they feel in your bodies.

D: Can they not see that good spirits inhabits our bodies and you influence them?

MG: They are attracted to you because you are clean because you are strong. That is more a challenge.

D: I am trying to put this into perspective. When I first came here the treatments the healer gave me were very helpful. Now you are saying this actually creates more problems for me now.

MG: He has helped you get rid of all those negativities from your body and we have helped him too. We have rid you of the remaining impurities. Now that you are pure, you do not need that any more. The people you take here, they do need him to help them get better.

If a person is susceptible, tired, angry, having different feelings, that person is very open to negative spirits. If you lie down there on the table and had a healing, there will be tiredness inside you. You will need to rest. At this moment when you feel tired, the negative spirit comes in before you can protect yourself.

Donald McDowall

FATIGUE AND LOSS OF CONTROL.

D: Is the message there for me never to be too busy where you cannot control what you do?

MG: That is true. We have always reminded you always to set aside something for yourself. These people (the healers) give everything. That is why they are exhausted. We are not saying that you should be selfish. You should always remember you could help others more if you are strong. If you give everything, you have nothing left to give. Even if you want to help more, you cannot help more, because you have nothing left. Always have a reserve.

HOW DETACHMENT WORKS

D: Can I help my friend do better with his life?

Master Gordon: Each has a life to live. You cannot live life for someone else. You take all opportunities to help, counsel, love, support, but this person is not a baby to be spoon-fed. The time is nearing for you to let go.

The key word here is "detachment". The other side is very pleased. We are disappointed.

D: We seem to be losing the battles Master Gordon.

MG: Eliminating excess baggage is the word. I would not be here with you if we were losing the battle. We only lose the battle if you side with the other forces. I would throw in the towel, leave you, and look for somebody else. We cannot let the negative forces win. He is helping us, at this time, to separate the weak from the strong.

These are hard lessons, and bitter medicine that must be taken.

D: What will happen to him next, Master Gordon?

MG: You will see him for what he truly is. He will be caught with his own lies, with his own baits. He even tried to fool his own guides.

D: How did he do that?

MG: There are times when his guide tried to communicate with him through his dreams. He would listen, nod and when awake he set the guide aside. That is what we mean by trying to fool his guide. He thinks the guide does not see and is not always there to see what he does. He is mistaken. Because he does not feel the guide's presence, he thinks the guide is not there. God is everywhere, all the time, in all circumstances. We sometimes deny His presence, but still He is there. Sure guides have limitations, but we are given the gift to be with you all the time.

DD: We appreciate that Master Gordon. Knowing God cares for us enough to help us, through you is very helpful and comforting.

MG: We will do our best to help each individual; until we cannot work with him any more, through his own choices. You have staff in your clinic, you give them freedom to move, to do and decide things, the best way to help patients and benefit the clinic. If one makes decisions contrary to rules, everybody is affected and you have to let that person go. You cannot work with that person any more.

It is the same with us. There are rules that have to be obeyed. There are freedoms as well, freedom of choices, for the best of everybody, not for selfish motives, or to hurt anyone. We have to let him go. I am sorry; sorry for him.

Do not be taken in. Those are his ways to pull a curtain so you will not see what goes on inside him. He is very adept at that. Play your cards close to your chest. Be careful. Protect yourselves. You are already on the defensive. When you should not be.

Again, you cannot work with people like this, people you cannot trust, people you cannot depend on to do what is right.

HOW ENERGY SURGES THROUGH THE BODY

D: Last night we were watching a movie about Excalibur and Annie saw an image of energy. This was about future beings in a submarine. Annie saw a man being punished with energy going through his body. She said that was similar to what she saw when I was healing.

Master Gordon: These are surges of energy, that is true. What she saw was an exaggerated version of the surge of energy that comes into your body while you are healing.

D: Where does this energy come from?

MG: Who gives you energy but God? You are manifesting energy in your body to give to a patient with a need. That is the reason why sometimes she tells you to give more, or lessen. She sees the need of the person.

D: Am I focusing energy better now?

MG: A word of advice: sometimes you forget yourself, just as your wife does. Reserve some energy for yourselves, especially you. You love people so much you give everything. Reserve some energy to give more to people. Give everything now and when you see an opportunity to help, there is nothing more to give. We are not saying you should turn your back on people, but you cannot give more if there is nothing left.

THE STRENGTH OF DETACHMENT

Master Gordon: Your friend's strength was also his weakness. Learn from this. He gave so much of himself he forgot he had a life of his own. Because of that weakness, people, his own children, took advantage. Let that be a lesson to you. Even with your patients, even with the people you will be meeting, reserve some energy for yourself. That is the meaning of detachment.

D: That is a hard lesson for me.

MG: All I have to do is think of God's will. I know that if I focus on that, I will not go wrong. Do the same. These are hard lessons, but to be indirectly responsible for other people taking advantage of you is harder. If you let them get a foot inside the door, this is welcoming them. Cut off the foot.

HEALING, FEAR AND FAMILY

D: A patient telephoned me yesterday to say he had hurt himself and he was in bed. He was afraid.

Master Gordon: Afraid of what?

D: Afraid of being in pain and being hurt. His family is helping him. I pray for him to get better quickly. He is a good man. Could you help him not to be afraid, and accept he will get better, and that he has to be patient?

MG: Fear comes with indecision, fear comes with doubt. Doubt in the goodness of God, doubt in the ability of God to heal. Inculcate that in him.

D: I will call him again today to help him.

MG: He has his family surrounding him, supporting him. In itself that is a manifestation of God's goodness. Some people have nobody and still trust God. He is in better circumstances.

HEALING THE HEALER

Master Gordon: How are you?

D: My toothache and headache are going away. I think I have made myself too tired.

MG: You are very like your wife. You know what is good, and still forget. Always have some reserves or you will not function properly. In your car you always carry a spare tyre and tools for fixing the car. You always have enough petrol, in the tank. Before the tank is emptied, you refill it. Do the same with you. Always have reserves.

D: We are learning this Master Gordon.

MG: You cannot help others if you are spiritually or physically weak. I am reminding you as well as your wife. There is time to speak and there is time to just keep quiet. She knows that very well and still she forgets.

You forget you have a physical body to take care of. In your profession you take care of both the spiritual man and his physical self. Remember you have a physical body to take care of too.

D: I will try to do better, Master Gordon.

MG: Yes, or you will have more aches and pains.

D: Thank you for your help and your strength.

MG: We are here to support you, to push you, to lift you up to attain the goal. We are a team. We cannot succeed if one is weak. We have to strengthen the weakness and be a support to the next fellow.

RECHARGING OUR BODIES WITH ENERGY

D: I looked at Annie through my mind the other night and saw blue electricity going through her body, from the centre out.

Master Gordon: We do the same thing with you, giving you a tune-up if you need it, change of oil if it needs a change of oil. That is what we do. That is what we do to everybody. That is what we will do for your children.

WHY WE GET HEADACHES

Jonah: Headaches are different physical manifestations. If you have an empty stomach and do a lot of work, you get headaches. If you have a lot on your mind and you feel overwhelmed, you get headaches. If your mind and heart do not agree, you get headaches and stomach aches.

D: Is this the same as Master Gordon explained about headaches?

J: We are talking of the physical here. There are also spiritual reasons.

THE ABUSE OF POWER

D: The U.S., the French and China are going to continue underground nuclear tests, I do not think we can change their minds. We are trying, but the French are very stubborn. When Jonah was telling us about the map he said that many other disasters would come from future nuclear tests. At that time tests were not being considered to any extent. Now the prospect is more dangerous.

Master Gordon: When Jonah spoke these words, you were not impressed. You had doubts. Each of us guides speaks two or three steps of time. When words are spoken, you cannot absorb these properly and try to resist. We acknowledge the limitation of man, but this is to show you of what is to come. When I speak with regards to your friend, or other future projects, I know resistance is there. I speak to prepare you not to have your hopes too high and despair later.

D: Thank you for your patience with us.

MG: There is also a breaking point how much we can tolerate. When I have had enough, I will tell you to stop.

D: Is there nothing that God can do to stop these people from bringing disaster?

MG: The choice is between good and evil and choices are made. They chose to display their power, not just physical power, but political and moral power over others, and they are drunk with a sense of power. You cannot reason with a drunken person; or with a drunken leader. They do not understand the ultimate consequences of their actions.

D: They expect to do this within the next year, Master Gordon. The process might be hastened in that time. If they conduct these tests in the next year, what will happen?

MG: Some more earth changes. Changes in nature as well, such as changes in living things. They are only hastening the process of evolution; evolution catastrophic in nature.

THE ABILITY TO BEND WITH PROBLEMS

Master Gordon: Be like the bamboo, bowing to the wind, then straightening up after the wind passes. Bending to the wind is the wise way, or you will break.

DETERMINING THE SOURCE OF MIRACLES

Master Gordon: What does he teach? Does he teach confusion? Does he teach doubt? You can see the results of what he does. That is why one should always be in tune with God and His work. The evil one can duplicate, to a certain degree, the works of God. You can judge by what is taught. If the intention is just to confuse, you must understand that. If the intention is to teach loving and honouring God, above everything else, you know that too.

You have written a book about psychic surgery and now you are working on a book touching on psychic surgery[11] [12]. Not all the psychic surgeons you went to are reliable. You have proven that. The real psychic surgeons teach goodness, faith and confidence in one's self. The others confuse and take money. The Devil can perform psychic surgery, to confuse and to take from others. Be warned.

(11) McDowall, D. A. Psychic Surgery – A Guide to the Philippines Experience. Australia: self-published; 1993
(12) McDowall, D. A. Healing-Doorway to the spiritual world. Self-published; 1998.

THE CONCEPT OF THE THIRD EYE

D: I have judged how much I should say to people and what I can do to give them the right amount of knowledge. This is getting easier. Some problems people have are much harder to work with. I can feel the difference when I am working now. I ask God for help and I feel the changes. The vision in my mind is different each time with each patient.

Annie and I came across the healer's references to the Third Eye and what he perceives when opening the third eye of his patients. He puts his finger on the forehead and tries to put in energy to help people develop it more easily. Annie was concerned we were giving people the wrong impression by describing this. We were confused about what the healer saw as the Third Eye and what we understood as the spiritual development given by God. Would you explain?

Master Gordon: When did she first discuss the Third Eye with you?

D: We have talked about this on and off for a long time, but never in depth like this. We wanted to make sure we had a clear understanding for the book. If the Third Eye was an energy centre, was the healer able to put in energy? Some say Buddhists try to open the forehead with minor surgery[13]. What does the healer see when he says their Third Eye is developing or open? How does this relate to how other people refer to the Third Eye?

MG: The healer was encouraging people to develop spiritual perception. This is an act of encouragement.

D: The Third Eye, as I understand then, illustrates a person's perception of the spirit world.

MG: Development depends on the person. No person can open or develop another's Third Eye.

D: Does the healer sense the person developing?

MG: He can sense an individual's development. Everybody has that ability. He cannot open the Third Eye for others. He can only encourage their ability to develop their own sense.

D: When he puts his finger on their forehead what happens?

MG: He was encouraging, conditioning for what the person should do. This is like a child starting to walk. The child is encouraged to do more until able to walk steadily. Those starting their spiritual development looked to the healer, as you did, and never question what he does. In some ways this encourages them to go on and continue with their beliefs. But this creates misconception of what goes on inside their bodies. This is very delicate. He can see himself as a god, or as an instrument to help others. There is a delicate balance.

D: Does that balance depend on a patient's need? Some need to respect the healer, others, when they talk with him, see him as an instrument.

MG: Not everybody has the same feeling. There are those who see through such healers. These healers cannot pretend to be anything else but themselves. Other people look up to them as demi-gods. They like this and the healers do not disillusion them.

(13) Lobsang Rampa T. The Third Eye – The Autobiography of a Tibetan Lama. Garden City, New York: Doubleday & Company Inc; 1957

A DIFFICULT HEALING PROBLEM, NEGATIVITY

D: Yesterday we worked with an old lady with cancer and tried to help her. We wanted to take all the dark, negative energy out of her, but this was very hard. What is stopping us from being able to do that?

Master Gordon: She is starting to doubt herself and her capability. That is very dangerous. Once she has that thought in her mind, she will go down. She may not own up to this, but this is in her mind, especially when she sees the lump on her neck.

D: Is there any way that we can help remove or reduce the lump?

MG: The lump is a symbol for her. She will not be safe while the lump is there.

D: Can you suggest how we might help her?

MG: Feed her with positive thoughts. Inspire her not to think of herself as she is now, but as she wants to be. That is the only way you can help her, along with constant praying and communicating with the Almighty.

D: She asked for more information to help. I told her she should read the New Testament, and gave her one of Jaime Licauco's books[14]. Are we blocking the way she should see things?

MG: What is bringing her down is that which is within her system.

D: Working with her is hard. I appreciate the help from Solomon and you. With Annie's help I will work with her every few days. The photographs her husband took might encourage her some.

(14) Licauco, J. T.   Exploring the Powers of Your Inner Mind. Makati, Philippines: Inner Mind Development Institute; 1992

A CASE OF BLINDNESS – HEALING AND FEAR

D: Yesterday we saw my friend who was blind. Annie said we might be able to do something for his eye. Did we do enough to help him?

Master Gordon: If he goes to the wrong person he will never get better. He will never regain sight in one eye.

D: We might have encouraged him a little. Is there anything else we should tell him?

MG: He has already accepted his blindness. He might not say this, but we know.

D: Many people when offered help fear being disappointed again. Does raising hope make a difference?

MG: If the person is willing.

LIMITS OF HEALING

D: Another patient also came for treatment yesterday. We were trying to help her more, to make her stronger. I tried explaining to her what I felt was happening to her.

Master Gordon: Helping is hard if the person is limited in absorbing the knowledge you are giving. She has to decide whether to accept what you teach her. We do understand that while she is with you she is accepting and open to all you teach her. After that, she falls apart, because there is nobody else to talk to and encourage her.

Do not be discouraged. Your responsibility is not to hold her hands every day. She has to stand up for herself. You can do only so much. She has a responsibility to herself. Do not be disheartened.

FEAR ATTRACTS EVIL

Master Gordon: Fear is the opposite of faith and trust in God. There should never be fear in your heart because that is the chance the evil one is looking for to take your guide from you.

The evil one comes because of fear. So remove fear from your mind, especially you and Annie, for your sake and for Solomon's sake.

You have given us your word. We all value this. We do not play lightly with you. We care a lot and will do all we can to help guide and care for you.

We are only limited by the choices you make. Think about what you say and do before it is too late.

Donald McDowall

WHY SOME PEOPLE KEEP THEIR CANCER

D: Master Gordon, my patient with the lump in her neck is coming today for treatments. I do my best to help her. If only I could reduce the lump in her neck as a sign for her. Her faith is not wavering, but becoming stronger. If the healers were not able to take that away, could there be a purpose for it being there? Is asking for that to be removed too much?

Master Gordon: She placed the irritation there herself. Healers, physicians, doctors can help only so much. If the patient is not willing to co-operate, you cannot do anything. She needs to complain all the time because in the past she always gave of herself. Now she is catching up with that. This is her way of asking people to look at her, give her attention, love. So she will not let go. She says she does, but she is scared to let go.

D: What do you mean?

MG: You have always asked God to give you the power to help others heal themselves. Now if you are given something you cannot control, it will control you. She asked, she prayed, and now she is scared because this lump is controlling her. This is why we only give you the power at different stages.

D: I do my best for her, Master Gordon, but I feel bad that healing people is restricted by my lack of development. This makes me sad.

MG: This is not your fault. She drains herself of all the positivity surrounding her. She could have saved this energy to strengthen herself. For her to enjoy her life she should have used the energy that you gave her. This is her choice. Every day you teach her to give more value to her life. But she does not seem to see this.

She is also very lonely. She could have used that energy to make herself feel more in control and not blanketed by loneliness. She

134

cannot blame you for her not getting well. Physically she is doing her best, but her heart and her mind resist. Do not let her drain you.

D: I gave her some books last time to help her understand her body. I hoped that they would help her be more responsible.

Today I will tell her the story about Oral Roberts and how he overcame his tuberculosis and learned his body still had to be strong even after healing[15].

MG: She has no trust. She asks God to heal her and God asks her to respond, but she does not because she is scared. How can she get better if she does not follow advice?

D: What did God ask her to do?

MG: What did you tell her to do? You are not God, but you are an instrument. Did she follow you completely, or did she follow you with one hand kept inside her pocket?

Tell her this is a slow process. If you tell her that healing starts from inside, she should understand that. Healing has responsibilities. She has responsibilities.

(15) Roberts O. Expect a Miracle, My Life and Ministry, Oral Roberts, An Autiobiography. Nashville, Tennessee: Thomas Nelson Inc; 1995

HOW TO APPROACH PROBLEMS

D: Thank you for visiting us Jonah. Today has been very trying for us, especially Annie. We are very concerned. The stress is heavy. All that is happening is having a very dramatic effect on our bodies.

Jonah: You open your arms to these problems. Do not entertain problems. Once you have solved a problem go to the next one, do not accumulate them. Solve problems while these are small and manageable. Then you seek help. Let this be a lesson. There will be problems. When something gives you trouble, remove it. Always have a clean slate. I am talking to you both, including this medium.

I speak strongly because you are awake. All the nerves in your body are awake and tingling. When you are half asleep you do not pay attention. Think of survival, not only of the group, but also of yourself, because you are the leader. You are sent to help everybody, not one group. You can help everybody by pointing to the truth and their responsibilities, not by solving their problems.

I have told you the bamboo sways with the wind. If you sway and bend with the wind the time will come when you stand straight again. A wise man follows the bamboo.

I have told you solving a problem close to you is very hard. That is why we are here. When emotions take over, there is disorder. Detaching yourself from a problem can be done. You are doing this. When you help yourself, you help your patients. If no one is thinking, everybody will be destroyed.

PREPARATION FOR MEDITATION

Jonah: Before meditating, pray. You heard how your friend here said an opening prayer.

Envelope yourself with white light, seek protection so you do not get frightened by your thoughts. The evil one will use every means to inject fear and doubt in your mind in different ways; He will use a person dressed as a beautiful package or an ugly package. This comes when you least expect it.

Every day when you wake, before bed and whatever you are doing, protect yourself with white light. Your meditation will flow freely. The spirit guide will come to you and be one with you. He will show you what you need and answer questions in your heart, in your mind, in your whole being. Share this with your friends.

USING CHARMS

D: Jonah, a few days ago I had a feeling I did not need to wear my necklace with the charms of Santo Ninó, and my little triangle around my neck. I took it off and put it on the shelf. Are having those things useful? Why was I prompted not to use or wear the pendants any more?

Jonah: In what circumstance did you get the pendants?

D: The Santo Ninó was given to me by a friend as a present. The pendant was very special for him. He wanted me to have the pendant to help me with my spiritual journey. The triangle was a present from the healer. The pendants were blessed by both those healers to bring good luck and help. I always wore these in honour of their caring for me, and to remind me of my mission and my purpose.

J: Did you feel anything when wearing the pendants?

D: I felt I should. There was no electricity, or any special feeling.

J: The child has reached puberty. You have outgrown these, as your wife said. You have seen their true value.

THE CURE FOR CONTROLLING EMOTIONS

D: Jonah what next should we prepare ourselves for?

Jonah: Your emotion is your second weakest point. You know your weakest point.

D: Chocolate.

J: This is no time for jokes.

You will perish if you use emotion for all problems. You will not be able to help people if emotion controls you. You should strengthen your commitment.

D: My life has always been like that, I am slowly learning with Annie's help.

J: In the past you easily got sick when upset.

D: I do not get sick so much any more. That is true.

J: You are learning the way. You are able to work more to produce more, and be able to better help others. You must be wise, not cruel, towards those needing you.

You need to detach yourself, or you will drown in your own emotions.

D: We are praying and meditating more, and the blessings are there, that is true. The tests are hard.

J: Back in school you had tests too. You passed them to go the next step. When you failed, you had to stay behind. It is the same with life. We have to add challenges to make life interesting, to strengthen the person. Let us not forget free will.

D: We appreciate your help. We see your hand and that of Master Gordon, and are aware of Solomon's help. We know that the path is still straight.

J: And I am honoured you are true to your word. As you progress, I progress too and Master Gordon progresses.

FEAR AND HAPPINESS

Master Gordon: What about your friend's health?

D: Can you predict how long my friend will live?

MG: We do not give exact dates. The time he has will be the most important part of his life, a time of extreme happiness. He has had his struggles, now is the time for him to have happiness.

Some grow very old without learning anything. Your friend started early and reaped the fruit early. His peak is the best time to harvest, when the fruit is sweetest. He should not be afraid. If he entertains fear, he is giving way for the evil one to work on him.

Fear is the enemy of faith. If he has faith he can trust completely in the goodness of God. If he has doubt, he has fear, and that erodes clarity of thoughts. He needs to strengthen his heart – Jonah has discussed this before – strengthen that emotion by seeing things for what they truly are. Then he can move forward. Emotions can be man's weak point.

As he travels this life, on the new road that we will show him, he will have a light journey, he should not tarry or he will never reach his goal. He knows how to step, he knows how to dance, so he should be light on his feet and all will be right.

WHAT TO TEACH OTHERS – THE FIRST STEPS

D: How would you summarise the lecture we gave tonight?

Master Gordon: Do you think that these people have learned how to pray, how to trust God? You should emphasise that first step. Work on that. This evening there were a few questions. Why do you think it is there? What is the reason for that? Like water to the sea. Learning how to pray was not easy for you. Teach them. Focus on trust in God's mercy and faith in Him. Teach people until they can hold their own.

DISCUSSION OF A DIFFICULT HEALING

D: A young man came yesterday who had a lot of pain in his back. I examined him but could not treat him because the pain was so bad. I silently asked God to bless him. He has something more seriously wrong with his back; I have asked him to get x-rays. He might have a growth or a disease. Do you know his problem?

Master Gordon: A growth is there. You cannot do anything. The growth is like having a decayed tooth, making the whole mouth tender or painful. No matter how much you want to help him, you cannot do much. You can encourage him to help himself. Prepare him emotionally. You can ease pain in other parts of his body, but this will be only temporary relief.

D: I will send him to a specialist medical doctor.

MG: Yes, to eliminate all other worries.

D: Master Gordon, some people I meet, I know I can help. Others believe God is going to perform a miracle to take away all their problems. When giving my lectures, how will I know, is there a sign or a feeling, which people have chosen to have a miraculous experience?

MG: In people's faces you will see fear, hope, or plain stubbornness. Those with fear you need to encourage. Those with hope, encourage those, too.

Those who accept defeat, you cannot help. People go to lectures to help themselves and get better. A few go there only to listen. Most go to seek help. You can distinguish what help they need. Basically words of encouragement, words of strength and that is healing the spirit, healing the emotions. You are very good at that.

The needy go to meetings. Observe them. Look into their faces. They wait for encouragement; they do not wait for miracles. They wait to be shown hope. The miracle they long for is the words of wisdom you can share with them. Of course, there are practical issues, like how to take better care of themselves, physically. These words can be given through books, pamphlets or other people.

These words of encouragement are the most important. How they can feel conflicts inside their heads and their souls. Dealing with physical pain is easy. But spiritual neglect is torment for everybody. That is what you will address.

WHICH PRAYERS ARE NOT ANSWERED

D: What should people understand when they pray?

Master Gordon: They should understand what their needs are. They do not always see how God answers their prayers, what the answer is and how they should be sensitive to that.

MG: Most people say their prayers are seldom answered. They are saying what they prayed for was not given and they have been given something else. But prayers are always answered.

Donald McDowall

ACKNOWLEDGING GOD

Master Gordon: Do not forget to pray before the lecture.

D: I did forget last time.

MG: Always acknowledge the presence of God, without Him there is nothing. With Him there is light, knowledge. As you pray before any meditation, pray again after the lecture to thank Him for the knowledge you were able to share with others.

D: We will do that, Master Gordon.

Were we able to get rid of all the negative entities in the home, or is there still more work to do?

MG: Like putting money in the bank, if you always withdraw, you will always be in the negative. If you keep saving, there will always be money in there. Here you are withdrawing the spirit and then taking the spirit back. Turn negative feelings into the constructive and positive.

They need encouragement. They must hear positive suggestions. If you want negative entities to leave, speak positively. Make room for positive thoughts in this house, instead of giving negative thoughts more room.

D: A long time ago you explained negative ones did not have access to our thoughts.

MG: That is correct, but you are speaking these thoughts. Not even I have access to those thoughts until they are spoken, or acted on. That is correct.

Negative thoughts grow bigger when acknowledged. Acknowledging positive thoughts gives less room to negative energy in this house.

D: What creates the negative and positive forces inside a person's mind?

MG: Fear. Love. Those are very basic. A child of four or five years breaks a toy. Either he will be scared to tell his parents or he knows he is loved and can tell his parents. The thought is in his mind. If he thinks his mother will spank him, or his father will not buy him a new toy, the problem will grow bigger and bigger until he learns to lie. If he knows he is loved, if he knows he will be listened to, he will be encouraged to say he is very sorry he broke this toy. This starts in the mind and continues through life. What we plant in the mind of the child becomes the same with grown-ups.

A DIFFICULT HEALING CASE – SELF-DISCIPLINE

D: My health is better, my energy is better, I understand more and I feel that I am helping people more. Sometimes there are those who have difficulties, and I do not understand why they do not respond so quickly, like the big lady. I know she is special and I know there is more I have to do with her, but her response was not as smooth as I expected. I have learned to be patient because, as a good teacher, you are going to give me challenging problems to work with.

Master Gordon: There are times encouraging people is better, and there are times when being firm is necessary. With this one you have to be firm. She is lax in self-discipline. Tell her you cannot work with her if she does not co-operate; not with words but actions. Tell her that her health is the concern and she should be more responsive to what you expect her to do. There are people who need to be encouraged, those who need to be inspired, and those who need to be threatened.

D: She has very strong attitudes about being threatened, Master Gordon.

MG: We do not mean physical threats, but you, the doctor, have the authority to tell her. You can discuss firmly with her. Remember, she would not be coming to you if she did not trust you. Ask why she keeps coming if she will not follow what you tell her. Tell her you need results.

D: I was much firmer with her this time.

MG: You can be firm and nice at the same time. Do not let her talk you into doing only what she wants. Tell her you are not happy with the slow progress. Tell her you could work better if she was more co-operative. Her body is her concern too. She should care more.

A CASE FOR HEALING – PERSISTANCE

D: Master Gordon, a woman called me yesterday. She had been told to call a friend who travelled with me on a visit to the Philippines and was healed of uterine cancer. This woman has cancer of the lung and bowel. Her condition has worsened. She was to have surgery and said she would contact me later. I told her I would pray for her. Is there is any advice I could pass on to help her? She was very despondent and had given up.

Master Gordon: There are two ways to be healed. One is through positive thinking, and you understand that well. The second is acknowledging the disease is serious and chopping off a little at a time she must start telling herself she is stronger than the disease. Physical healing starts working if she tells herself she will not succumb, but will overcome the disease.

She has been despondent; with a few words from friends that depression, that dependency could be lifted and would strengthen her spiritually. Not just by you; by family and friends who live with her. She could gain strength. Acknowledging a deadly disease is a step she has taken. Acknowledging the disease as stronger than herself is not good.

D: She overcame her bowel cancer five years ago, and suddenly finds this when she thought she was stronger. This is hard.

MG: Life is a constant battle. She should never give up. She should acknowledge the condition and respond accordingly. You acknowledged the condition, but what matters is what is being done.

Donald McDowall

THREE QUESTIONS FOR CANCER PATIENTS

Master Gordon: There are three questions to ask the people that have cancer, or other diseases. Do they recognise the seriousness of their condition? Do they want to overcome the condition? Do they accept death? How they answer these questions tells you whether they will survive.

ANOTHER CASE FOR HEALING – CHANGE

D: A lady we treated yesterday had difficulty hearing. I asked Annie if we could help her. The woman is very faithful, comes to the lectures and tries hard to get better. Is there anything else we can do to help her?

Master Gordon: Your wife has taught her a prayer. The woman has always been scared all her life. Losing one of the senses is scary indeed. Imagine losing the sense of sight, or movement. She has become defenceless. This woman has been battered all her life; spiritually, emotionally, and physically.

She needs to learn to fight back, fight for her rights. Fighting back can start her thinking for the future. She should change, maybe, her profession, if she is a professional. She can change her house. Even a change of perspective will help. She can do this gradually. She can also change her doctors.

Until she finds an effective means of helping herself that is the best you can do for her.

Donald McDowall

ANOTHER CASE STUDY – OVERFEEDING

D: I have a male patient who has a bad back. He plays bowls and bends over a lot. Many doctors have worked with him. I feel he does not respect what I am doing for him. I do not think I have got what is necessary for him. Can I help in a more beneficial way, or am I doing as much as I can at the present?

Master Gordon: Overfeed a child and the child will only waste the food given him. This man is but a child, at this stage.

He is learning; he listens, let that be your guide. Time will come when he will ask for more. You can then give him what he needs. You cannot give him everything at once, or all will be wasted.

D: I do not want to give up. That is why I want to help him.

MG: Invite him to your lectures. He will learn there. You cannot spend a whole morning or afternoon discussing spiritual healing with him.

SWITCHING OFF THE ENERGY

D: Why is my face red at times?

Master Gordon: That is energy flowing inside you. You do not switch off and there is redness in your face. Learn to switch off.

D: How do I switch off?

MG: After work, or after each healing, switch off, and then use the energy again when needed. Having the feeling being available at all times is pleasant, but you should know when to turn on and off.

D: I will pay more attention.

MG: That is why you tire so easily.

D: What is the easiest way to switch off?

MG: After each healing, you say thank-you to God for helping you, ask your angel to help you, go back to your old self. They will do that. Rather like coming out of the water after a swim, drying yourself. Ask and energy will be given to you.

You are enjoying that flow of energy, but be economical.

Donald McDowall

THE NEXT STAGE OF HEALING – CONTROLLING THE CHARISMATIC PERSONALITY

Master Gordon: The goal of the guide is to assist humans to temper some of their ambitions. This soldier the guide is working with is very charismatic with his words and his physical self. Jonah has to temper these ambitions. It is the same with you. It is easy to use sexuality and emotions to communicate. But it can give the wrong impression. People might pursue you for your body, not for your spiritual strength and counselling.

D: I can see the wisdom in focusing emotions and energies to be more sensitive to the spiritual side of people. The value of communication appears to be much greater with people responding to instruction or suggestion.

MG: Be careful when touching some people. Touching can be interpreted as caressing and gives a different value. Be supportive but be aware that others think differently than you do.

HEALING AT THE LAST MINUTE

Master Gordon: Some people come at the last stages and then healing is not easy. Say this in your lecture. Before the disease takes control, they should rest, see a doctor and follow the doctor's advice. A condition must not be buried.

D: Why do people not act until the last minute?

MG: They are scared or do not value themselves. They neglect themselves. Everyone must take care of their bodies for them to function correctly.

Donald McDowall

THE ILLUSION OF BEING YOUR BROTHER'S KEEPER

D: We were brought up to be our brother's keeper. That is a hard lesson to ignore.

Master Gordon: To be a brother's keeper does not mean you should feed him all the time. He will become a spineless parasite.

Each person has a mission. You cannot always be ensuring another's mission. You can only teach them through example. If they learn something from you, well and good. That is all. Do not live their lives for them.

DO PEOPLE KNOW WHAT THEIR SPIRITUAL GIFTS ARE?

Master Gordon: Some people recognise gifts given them, others do not know what to do with their gifts.

Ask them to ask themselves what they are good at, if they are using what they have. Some use their hands for painting. Some have a gift of preaching. Some have a gift with healing, some with helping others progress. Ask if they recognise their gifts and how they use them.

Donald McDowall

PHYSICAL DEFORMITIES ARE CAUSED BY THE EVIL ONE

D: Why are some people joined together at birth?

Master Gordon: Two people attached to one another with one dominant and the other a parasite is not normal. One bows down to the wishes of the other. The weaker one can accept or not. But they both are their own person physically.

The evil one surely works in many ways to create havoc.

D: Are physical deformities because of the evil one?

MG: God creates beauty, not monstrosity. The evil one uses power, creating deformity.

The evil one uses his power to create uncertainty. All means are used.

There are doctors who exploit or experiment on humans. Sometimes their work does not necessarily benefit humanity. There are side effects from many chemicals commonly used. You must always be sincere. Humility in knowledge and power will get you a long way.

MATHEW MANNING – THE GUIDE'S IMPRESSION

D: We went to listen to Mathew Manning, considered the greatest psychic in Europe and England[16]. What was your impression of his work?

Master Gordon: I am repeating what he said: be spontaneous in healing, always be ready to reach out, always be prepared to help. This is vital for a person's development. Rituals are man-made and are not important for helping people. A person should prepare to be helpful all the time. You do that through discipline and constant search for the light. A person taking being blessed and strengthened for granted does not work. A person needs to always be in touch with a spirit guide and with God.

D: Who helps this man, Master Gordon? Mathew Manning, of all the healers that I have met, had the attitude most similar to those we had been working with. I had not seen anybody else who had developed to that extent. As he said, he had a struggle within himself before his direction became clear.

He said that he had his closest experience with God when he was in the mountains. He was given two messages: to follow his own intuition and not be influenced by other people's demands of him, and to pursue the direction of a healer.

Does that mean he heard his guide, did you help him, or was that an experience he had with God?

MG: The spirits are everywhere. God is everywhere. People travel the world looking for God, looking for happiness, for peace, when in reality they are always with him. Man has to wake up to that reality. This man did that. He wanted to find God, so he travelled. He found God is everywhere. He found Him in himself at that time. That was his wake-up call.

Have you not yet realised your wake-up call?

Donald McDowall

(16) Manning, Mathew. Mathew Manning's Guide to Self Healing. Thorson's Publishing Group. Kent, England, 1989.

NOT ALL PATIENTS ARE FOR ONE DOCTOR

D: There are people from different walks of life, among them are derelicts that have lost all hope and there are also the drug-addicts. They are all different people. There are many angry at the world and destroy their bodies with that anger.

Master Gordon: Tomorrow you will find someone like this on your doorstep. Do not get wholly involved. This would be very dangerous.

D: Somebody on drugs, Master Gordon?

A few weeks ago somebody like this came. I got a headache and I did not accept this person as a patient for some reason. I felt I was getting a message from Solomon this person was not for me.

MG: Such people create problems. You are not the right doctor for them.

D: I learned that lesson a long time ago.

MG: This one will be different. This person will be tugging at your emotions. I am cautioning you now. Turning away a patient is not easy, especially one who is in need. You have to or you will be blackmailed emotionally. You will put yourself in danger. Detach yourself. This is not for you.

D: I will be cautious.

MG: Do not even refer this person to other doctors working with you.

D: Thank you for warning me, Master Gordon.

MG: Caution your staff. They have trained their eyes to see. Tell them if they see somebody who does not fit in, be gracious, but send them away.

D: Should I tell the staff before or after?

MG: Caution them that just in case somebody comes in. Tell them this is a chiropractic clinic, not a rehabilitation centre. Tell them about your past experiences with some of these people. Tell them that the clinic could not help them. They should be gracious, but firm. They are the first people these derelicts will encounter before they reach you and the other doctors.

They have trained their eyes; they are not silly, they will know. Do not alarm them. Tell them casually to be cautious.

HEALING ENERGY

D: I notice that now as I am working, the strength coming into my body and my hands is much greater. Am I more sensitive, or is more being given?

Master Gordon: The answer is both. You are more awake, more aware of what is going on around you, and more is being given you. More responsibilities are also being given. The more power you are given, the more responsibility you have.

D: I want to help these people to achieve what they want in their lives. Some have damaged their bodies so much over the years and I think I do not have what they need. I give them as much as I can and then ask God to bless them.

MG: You cannot do everything for them at once. I cannot give you everything in one meeting, in one discussion. Your body will not be able to take too much and your mind will not be able to absorb everything. This would be very overwhelming. It is the same with you and your patients.

ETHICS OF MEDICAL EXPERIMENTS

D: We read a story about people who have visions. One doctor had devised a helmet using magnets and different voltages of electricity, to activate parts of the brain for people to have visual experiences of God[17]. He explained that parts of the brain trigger these experiences. Anybody can have these experiences if that part of their brain is activated. My understanding is this is a doorway into the next world. What scientists perceive as an hallucination or an illusion can be the doorway. Has he found a way to activate the brain without a person having to train their brain to do this?

Master Gordon: This is very dangerous. The evil one can use this to deceive man.

Discovering there is a portion of the brain that can be activated is acceptable, but to work without proper guidance and moral ethics is dangerous. This is a way of controlling man and will be used by the evil one to do so. They have already started planting particular messages in the brain to control man. The atom bomb was at first a wonder, next a cause of horror and destruction.

D: Is this why working under God's guidance with the creative energy is important?

M: If man has too much power or has too many discoveries, he would not know how to use these properly. Man can get drunk with too much power and then creates havoc among his fellow man. He needs proper guidance. This is war.

D: Is this why Solomon's coming is so important?

MG: This is war and we need a leader. Man is at a crossroads. At times he is confused, at times he knows what he is doing. We need a leader to pull us all together, and to show us the way. War started many years ago. The evil one will use anyone, any form and any way for man's destruction. Do not be deceived by this discovery.

(17) Motluk, A. Seized by God. New Scientist, Vol 172, No 2317, Page 20. Nov 17, 2001.

Donald McDowall

WORKING WITH GOD'S GIFTS

D: Why did this healer not develop his gifts further?

Master Gordon: This man was forced, willingly, by his wife, to become a healer because this was an easy job for both of them. They were able to travel and be received. They did not improve. When given a gift, you only do not accept, but improve the gift to help more people. Making money is secondary. The gift is to help others relieve their emotional and physical pain.

Use the gift to make dollars and the gift will go. His friend who abused the gift lost his power. That is why we have always been strict with you. You will learn the true value of these gifts.

HELPING DOCTORS

D: Master Gordon, we gave our lecture to my friends. Talking to your best friends about how they can improve their work is not easy. I did the best I could. Did they absorb the message?

Master Gordon: Yes. You should have been more direct. You were talking to your best friends. You could have been more direct and asked them if at times they felt their energy running out and they were low, emotionally, physically, mentally, what they did? Did they get angry, or did they escape from those causing them stress? Some of them felt you had dropped your profession and embraced only healing.

Your profession is the centre of discussion. You are trying to better understand man, not merely physically, emotionally, mentally, but spiritually.

Where do you go, what do you reach out for when you feel empty inside, when you think that you have reached your limit of understanding, your limit of giving to your patients? Do you have a bank that you can dip into? What is that bank of reserves? Spiritual energy is that bank of reserves.

Most important is the physician. If his energy is restored, he can give more to his patients. The happier he is in himself, the more productive he is.

Before making a speech, practice on your wife, or in front of a mirror. Good speakers do that.

Putting your thoughts into writing is not sufficient. Speak out loud. Hear yourself and prepare for questions.

All this is preparing for when you will be out there, preaching. It will be different from talking to your own kind. Make them the centre of the discussion. You do this with your patients.

Talking to a group of magicians, you put them in the centre of the discussion and build your topic around them.

You were nervous and that is why you should practice. Rehearse, practice, crystallise thoughts. This gives you more strength.

D: Was it enough for a beginning for them, Master Gordon?

MG: To some, yes; others, were unsure of you. They were uncertain if you had given up chiropractic and completely embraced healing; or whether you incorporate the two. You should make clear that chiropractic is your main concern, healing is incidental.

D: Should I write a summary to make this clear for them?

MG: Do not use too many words. That would only confuse. Speaking more directly makes understanding clearer. They want to know what is in your heart.

MG: The old man understood what you were saying. He read more into what you said.

You were saying man should not focus only on the physical, but open up his mind to something powerful to be discovered. He knows that.

He believes in the spirits, he believes in the strength, he believes in God. The other doctors have started to forget. Some were not sure and some were afraid to know. That is why you should be more direct. Make chiropractic the centre of the discussion. Then you can apply your other knowledge. Write your summary in this way to them.

NEGATIVITY AND MEDITATION IN NEW PLACES

D: The other night we meditated in the pyramid. When Annie's turn came, she had a pain in her chest. What was happening to her?

Master Gordon: I do not understand the question. When meditating, you should feel nothing because your mind expands. She was not meditating properly or not at all.

Donald McDowall

TAKING CARE OF GOD'S GIFTS OF HEALING

Master Gordon: All were given opportunities to use the gift, like an inheritance. How you invest is your choice. You can share with others, and invest some in business.

Everything goes with the gift, even money. If you do not use the gift properly, you will not be taken care of. All gifts have responsibilities. You have those responsibilities.

You have gifts, you have extra gifts, but you have to take responsibility for these.

D: I do my best, Master Gordon.

MG: In marriage, you have pleasure and also have responsibility. Each partner has been given rights and responsibility. The water has dried up.

D: What do you mean the water has dried up, Master Gordon?

MG: Other healers misused the gifts they were given. No matter how hard they try, the gifts will never come back.

He should not do psychic healing any more. Doing so will cause him public humiliation. Not everybody witnessing healing believes. They may be quiet for a while, but will speak out. Some are waiting for the opportunity. One of them will challenge him.

D: Is his magnetic healing still helpful, Master Gordon?

MG: No, this is a placebo.

People feel what they want to feel. Some are realists, feeling pain.

D: One woman felt pain during the surgery. I had never seen that before. In all the other surgeries I have seen there was no pain.

MG: There should be no pain at all. That is an indication to you.

Explain this to others, or they might come to you confused.

UNDERSTANDING BACK PAIN

D: I want my back to be stronger. Master Gordon.

Master Gordon: Your back will never be strong if you do not take precautions.

A person spends at least six hours in bed. Posture when you are working is important. Do you take enough rest? Do you feel lying on a chiropractic table is better than lying in your bed? More water is needed to firm the waterbed to support your back. A soft bed has not enough support. Weak necks need firm braces. You need a firm bed for your back.

First this will not be comfortable, but will work for you. Make sure your bed is firm, and do not forget your working posture. We will do the rest. The problem here is physical.

PREPARING TO HEAL – ACCEPTANCE

D: Master Gordon this week a colleague wrote to me about a friend with cancer. He asked if we could help. Is accepting people so ill right at this time?

Master Gordon: This is a test for you. You must decide in each case. The patient must have acceptance. Giving complete healing is hard if the disease has spread. You can help him have more quality for his remaining life, and you can release some of his pain. There are limits to what you can do. You can support him in his acceptance.

It is important he accepts death and what he has made of life. Do not promise what you cannot deliver. He will be one of many coming to you. Another patient is coming. Keep a safe distance from this one for the first few days. His mind is explosive. He does not know what to do with himself. If you go near too quickly, he might suck your energy all at once. Give him enough of that support you are capable of giving. Distance yourself. You have to protect yourself, because this person will be rather demanding. If he sees you are willing to help, he will cling like a leech.

You will not be able to balance yourself if you give everything to one.

THE LECTURES AND BALANCE OF HEALTH

D: Master Gordon, do you have any suggestion about the next lecture I will be giving?

Master Gordon: Always make clear you are concerned with physical and spiritual health, balanced by man's emotional self. You do not control the future of the individual.

D: I see the balance there, Master Gordon.

MG: Your lectures should not depend completely on pictures. Pictures are helpful as a necessary tool. The more pictures you show them, the more they might ask you that which is not consistent with the lectures. They might divert the lecture into something different. Pictures are to help understand what is going on, but are not the centre of discussion.

Some go to the lectures for supernatural insight. They could read the wrong signals. Keeping focused would help. I will talk with them, if this would help.

TEACHING PATIENTS TO PRAY WHILE HEALING

Master Gordon: You should teach them to pray. All will work out better if they know how to pray for themselves.

D: If I sense they are open, I suggest they pray. Should I do more?

MG: Do not use too much of your energy if they can use their energy. They should help themselves get better and not depend only on the doctor. The two should work together. The responsibility is not only the doctor's.

WHY SOME PEOPLE DO NOT GET BETTER AS QUICKLY

D: As I work with the patients, I see some who do not get better as quickly as others.

Master Gordon: They are comfortable and familiar with what they have. Getting better is foreign to them. They are not good at changing.

There are those who wait for others to make changes for them, when they should be making changes themselves. They have grown used to how they are. There are those who travel light, easily shifting from one place to another. Healing is there, but if not held on to it becomes useless. A pen has no purpose unless it is used. Kept in the pocket, a pen only occupies space. In the hand for writing, the pen serves a purpose. Do not blame yourself if some people do not get better. Some people just take time to accept, but healing is there; the knowledge is there. These two are the individual's decision. Do not feel you are a failure.

D: Do I need do more? When I know they should be getting stronger but are not, I feel frustrated.

MG: Each one has choices. A pen can be used, thrown away, or put in a box.

D: My intention is to keep improving my skills, improving, improving, and finding better ways to help people.

MG: Do not blame yourself if people choose to put this healing in a box. You will be wasting energy you can use elsewhere.

PREPARING THE PATIENT FOR THE HEALER

D: Some people have been asking who to visit and where to go for healing. I discussed with Annie if we were ready to accept these people now – or give them their choices of going to the places they are asking about.

Master Gordon: Give them the choices. Tell them what to expect. The responsibility is their's. Make it clear they should be responsible for their decisions. This is out of your control.

You control only things that you have access to. If they go to this healer that is really out of your control. You should be happy for them if they decide to go. If they decide to stay with you, you should accept. There is no guarantee they will be healed. It is their acceptance that is needed. Even if they go to a regular doctor and do not follow the doctor's advice, they will keep spending money and not get better. There is no guarantee they will be healed.

Healing depends on the seriousness or stage of their illness when they go to a healer. There are those who need more spiritual healing, or reconstructing. Others are easily encouraged and independent. Watch out for those who try to take more energy than they can use. Explain this in your lectures.

Donald McDowall

REST, ACCEPTANCE AND HAPPINESS

Master Gordon: Even God has a holiday. You are free today, but make sure you have enough rest. One of your friends needs some counselling, but he is too proud to say.

D: What is the message for him, Master Gordon?

MG: There are times when he needs to free himself of what is binding him. He has to be happy with what he wants, with what he does, with his decisions, or to accept what is there.

A person can be happy with what is available, or seek what is truly wanted. Acceptance is a prerequisite for happiness. Longing for what is not there, makes things worse. I will give you an example. Do you know what is inside your refrigerator?

D: Generally, yes.

MG: Okay. When you are hungry do you have any particular thing you want to eat? For example, every morning I see you eating the sandwich. If you are home, do you think you can prepare the same food from what you have inside your refrigerator, or do you have to prepare a different kind, based on what you have available?

D: I use what is there.

MG: The same thing with your friend. Either he has to rely on what is available for him and be contented with that, or get dressed and go to the restaurant and order what he wants. A person can be happy with what he has available, or he can go out of his way and seek what he truly wants. Unless a person is happy with himself, with his decisions, with what he wants, he will never feel better. Acceptance is one prerequisite towards happiness. Longing for something that is not there will only make things worse, unless you are willing to go out and seek it.

HEALING THE HEALER – DETACHMENT AND MEDITATION

Master Gordon: You should be resting yourself, meditating. I know you pray many times a day, but seldom have time to meditate and relax, to make yourself stress free and available to the spirits. Your body is taxed with all these activities.

Stress is your enemy. You have a lot of patients and a lot of love, a lot of understanding. But you have to rest and meditate for us to be able to remove that stress from you and your body.

You work hard each day to help others help themselves. Now is your turn to help yourself. Lie down and meditate, not just fall asleep. We could help you rid yourself of that neck condition.

D: I know my lot has always been to experience what I teach best to others. This in God's wisdom, must be the best way for me.

MG: You have aches and pains because you are sensitive to your patients. You empathise with your patients. Do not bring their problems and negativities into your life. One way of lessening that is by tuning off after each healing. Feeling while you are healing is understandable, but you cannot give everything. You will not last the day, or even the morning. Detach yourself from negative feelings.

Donald McDowall

PATIENT STORY – PARTNER DEPENDENCY

D: Is the man we went to see yesterday better now, more comfortable?

Master Gordon: As far as his body can take, yes. His body is worn out, he is old, and he is stressed. He is wondering if he is dying or has a disease. A body cannot take such stress. That is why he is suffering.

D: We did our best to relax him and help him, Master Gordon.

MG: You should relax the wife more. The husband feels what he sees in his wife, and what the wife sees in her husband makes her more nervous. This is a cycle between the two of them. That is how close they have become. Each is dependent on the other. They are one.

D: We will work with them to make them better, Master Gordon.

180

HEALING THE HEALER – PART 2

Master Gordon: How is your back?

D: I slipped in the shower yesterday and hurt my back. I was angry with myself for doing that. I was not careful enough. My back is getting better now.

MG: How is your neck?

D: That is getting better, too. Both are getting better slowly.

MG: You tell your patients to relax, take things easier, rest. Why can't the doctor apply this to himself? Take your own advice. Do you not consider yourself a doctor for yourself? You are still a human being with all the frailties.

You will not be able to work if you do not give yourself time to rest. Even at home you work two-thirds of the time. Take it easy at least once a week. Just relax, enjoy yourself, and enjoy each other's company. You will find out you are enjoying yourself.

That is why you are feeling all these aches and pains. Even when you are asleep, before sleeping you work. Give yourself some time to play, or to just relax.

D: I thought I was increasing my rest time.

MG: When you are home, you still work. When you go to bed you read, and those readings are not relaxing. You are attached to your mobile phone. You are attached to your computers. Switch off every now and again. Switch yourself off work, even for a few minutes.

Tonight you had a laugh or two. That is very important, relaxing, having a laugh. That is a release. Do not work at relaxing. Relaxing has to be spontaneous. You need to make an appointment with yourself to relax. Get yourself a book and make an appointment there. This is like telling yourself you need to make an appointment with God. God is not like that; you do not need an appointment to reach Him. But with yourself, you need to make an appointment.

How will your guide help you if you are always tied down to your work, or are too tired. Not only now you having closeness with your guide. He will need to be physically close to you. How can you do that when you do not even have time to spare for yourself?

People visit friends and give them what they call quality time. What is quality time? Making an appointment with others? You get more stressed because you consider that work as well, because you have to put in this kind of quality – whatever quality you mean – into a specific time, and that is also work.

D. D. PALMER

D: While researching, I found that old DD Palmer *[the discoverer of modern chiropractic]* said he talked to a spirit called Dr Jim Atkinson[18]. Is this accurate? Is there another story?

Master Gordon: At that time spirits were not well received. They were confused with the evil ones. People then were not well informed. This man used the name of a doctor to express his spiritual knowledge, so that those listening to him would accept him. You say Dr McDowall because this has more weight than Donald. The title carries more authority. He was doing the same. He was talking to his guide and had permission to use the title. He then had the ears of the people around him, instead of being rebuked. He would have been burned at the stake if he said his spirit guide told him what to say.

Even his son would not expose that side of his father's discovery to the public. He feared their discovery of chiropractic would be destroyed. He feared his standing in society would crash to the ground. That is why he had conflicts with his father. He believed in chiropractic, but did not tell people. The other man was very strong in his beliefs.

Your colleagues know chiropractic is effective in healing the patient, but do not say so in public for fear of being criticised by other professions. They hide it under the guise of technology.

(18) Palmer D. D. Textbook of the Science, Art and Philosophy of Chiropractic for Students and Practitioners. Portland, Oregon: Portland Printing House Company; 1966. Page 98

RULES FOR HEALING

D: God has the ability to heal and you have this ability too. The healing has to be through a physical medium. Others can witness that healing. Sometimes people pray and get better. Sometimes they do not pray, keep doing their work, and get better. Sometimes a lot of people pray for a person they do not know and that person gets better. Some people have to go to different places and healers and accumulate knowledge before there is any change. Are there rules for these procedures, or is this random?

Master Gordon: They must have faith in themselves and in the strength of their convictions. Some have faith in themselves, faith in others, or faith in the Almighty. Faith works in helping them get better. If they do not have the faith, people around them have the faith. That is why they are cured. When they get healing, doubts in their minds are erased. They have the strength of conviction of those around them.

Guides need a medium, or somebody to mediate for them. People might be scared at seeing something floating in front of them without somebody explaining to them. We have to use a medium to reach others.

Lucifer assumed he was as powerful as his maker, and he challenged God. This is dangerous for any man to assume. That is why we use others to reach out.

We scold you to help you recognise somebody is more powerful than you. Pride will start to rule and that would not be good.

There are already people stopping to hear you. There will be many tools for you to reach them. People will come to listen and you will be using these influences on them. Put discipline in that knowledge. Some might misinterpret, or you might forget from where knowledge comes. You need perspective to communicate this knowledge.

THE POWER OF THE MIND

D: What is the mind capable of?

Master Gordon: Everything. The mind is a very productive thing and a very dangerous thing too. That is why you have all this chaos around. That is why you have all these preachers around. That is why you have all these do-gooders around. The mind is limitless; to a point.

It can learn by listening to its own conscience, or it can learn to listen to the evil one. Either case needs discipline because without discipline, the mind would be like a short-circuited wire. Why do you think you have the aeroplane, for example? Why do you have a refrigerator? Why do you have a broom? They all exist because of man's needs. Invention comes out of those needs. The mind invents.

Why do you have war? Why do you have famine? Because someone's mind short-circuited and was used in the wrong way. How did you send these people to outer space? It is the mind. You have a quest for that knowledge; it is a quest for what is out there, the unknown. Why do you have all these books? To document all that knowledge, so people will not forget.

You have all the materials; what you have to learn is how to use it constructively, and you can do that with discipline. And that is one of the reasons why we have these conversations with you, why we discipline you at times. We do this to help you. It is not just for your personal needs, but so you can help others.

A PATIENT STORY – EMPTINESS

D: There was a lady, who came to see me, and she wanted to know her purpose. I tried my best to help her. I explained to her that she should list the things that she felt were her qualities and another list of her desires, then look at those and see if something comes out. I told her that I would ask you about her because she has the time and the freedom to pursue what God wants her to do. She said she would make any sacrifice to fulfil that purpose. Was there a purpose that I could tell her that would help her some more?

Master Gordon: If she said she has the time and if she is strong enough then she should work with the elderly, because there are many old people around who are neglected. They are dumped into nursing homes with nobody to really comfort them. She can go and visit with them, talk with them, read, be there as a companion. She can try that for a start and then from there she will find herself; she will find what she is looking for. It does not follow that she will stay there for the rest of her life, but that is how she will find her heart, as to what her heart is telling her. She can try that for a few days. In two or three days she will know. But as it is, it is all vacant.

D: What do you mean, "it is all vacant"?

MG: Her mind, her heart, is vague. Once she gives a little of herself to others, and these are very needy people, she will find what she wants with herself, a fulfilment of her being. She will find her talent; whether it is in teaching crafts, or it is in telling stories, meaning she can go to the theatres and help. Whether it is missionary work, whether it is to care. People who are confused with what their purpose is need to give of themselves freely. So she should try this. If it does not work she can find another area, but she will find this very uplifting.

A PATIENT WITH STROKE

D: One of my patients had a stroke. I was worried for him if there was anything we could do for him, or if in time he will heal?

Master Gordon: This is the time he will be finding himself.

D: He has had a hard life Master Gordon.

MG: Like an ostrich, a hard life running and putting his head in the sand at the same time. Now this is time for facing himself in the mirror. He will be confused, but then the calm in his life will come and when that time comes, he will find peace inside himself.

D: So this is only temporary for him? He will recover?

MG: Yes, but it will take a lot of time recovering, and that process will help him become a better individual. He needed this as a wake-up call. Some people need adversities to wake up to what they are doing to themselves, and he is one of these people who needs a big jolt to assess himself for what he truly is capable of doing.

D: At the moment his memory is gone.

MG: He is spinning like a top. But he will find his soul. What is the body for but a vessel for the spirit? If the spirit is not happy, if the spirit is not healthy, of what use is the body? This is a critical point in his development.

D: Should we visit him and help him, or is it something that he needs to –

MG: If you visit him at this time it will be useless. Give him time. You can visit him in a few months, or a few weeks time, but not now; it will not serve much of a purpose. You can visit with the wife or with the relatives. But visiting the man will be of no use to him. You can show your concern though, to the family.

D: Mmm, we will do that.

Donald McDowall

REFERENCES

(1) Nelson K. Edgar Cayce's Hidden History of Jesus. Virginia Beach, Virginia; 2000.

(2) Fuller J. G. Arigo: Surgeon of the Rusty Knife. Frogmore, St Albans, Herts, England: Granada Publishing Ltd; 1977

(3) Martin H. J. III. The Healing Ministry of Jesus Christ. Makati, Philippines: Loyal Printing; 1986

(4) Arigo: Surgeon of the Rusty Knife. John G. Fuller, Crowell Co, New York, 1974.

(5) The Practice of the Presence of God, Conversations & Letters of Brother Lawrence. Oxford, England: Oneworld Publications; 1993

(6) Kirkwood A. Mary's Message of Hope. Nevada City, CA: Blue Dolphin Publishing Inc; 1995

(7) Parrallel. Strange Talents. Music from beyond the grave, Page 24-27. Orbis Publishing, 1995

(8) Manning M. The Strangers. Vale, Guernsey, C. I.: The Guernsey Press Company Ltd; 1995

(9) [VIDEO] Savalas T. Channeling Voices from Beyond. Distributed by Eagle Entertainment Australia & New Zealand; 1991.

(10) Valentine T. Psychic Surgery. New York, New York: Pocket Book; 1975

(11) McDowall, D. A. Psychic Surgery – A Guide to the Philippines Experience. Australia: self-published; 1993

(12) McDowall, D. A. Healing-Doorway to the spiritual world. Self-published; 1998.

(13) Lobsang Rampa T. The Third Eye – The Autobiography of a Tibetan Lama. Garden City, New York: Doubleday & Company Inc; 1957

(14) Licauco, J. T. Exploring the Powers of Your Inner Mind. Makati, Philippines: Inner Mind Development Institute; 1992

(15) Roberts O. Expect a Miracle, My Life and Ministry, Oral Roberts, An Autiobiography. Nashville, Tennessee: Thomas Nelson Inc; 1995

(16) Manning, Mathew. Mathew Manning's Guide to Self Healing. Thorson's Publishing Group. Kent, England, 1989.

(17) Motluk, A. Seized by God. New Scientist, Vol 172, No 2317, Page 20. Nov 17, 2001.

(18) Palmer D. D. Textbook of the Science, Art and Philosophy of Chiropractic for Students and Practitioners. Portland, Oregon: Portland Printing House Company; 1966. Page 98

INDEX

A

absent healing, 88
acceptance, 173, 177, 178
accident, 54
accidents, 36, 54, 92, 102
adversities, 187
alcohol, 72
alike spirits, 40
Amish, 44
angels, 1
anger, 72
Arigo, 41, 42, 58, 94, 189
atom bomb, 164
aura, 99
awareness, xiv, xvi, 2, 9, 103

B

baggage, 71, 115
balance, 1, 15, 67, 80, 99, 128,
174, 174
bamboo, 125, 136
battles, 19, 115
beacon, 80
beliefs, 1, 8, 9, 13, 42, 73, 128,
183
Bible, xiii, 8, 23, 25, 71
blackmailed, 161
blindness, 131
Book of Mormon, 9
bowel cancer, 149
brain, 164
Brazil, 58, 94
brothers, 74

C

casino, 39
casinos, 39
chain-smokers, 70
change, 8, 33, 36, 40, 42, 77,
103, 121, 123, 151, 184
chaos, 185
character, 1, 2, 3, 4, 60, 86,
103
charms, 138
Chief White Feather, 55
child, 74, 84, 86, 91, 92, 95,
128, 138, 147, 152
children, 48, 49, 50, 51, 74,
118, 121
chiropractic, 70, 92, 162, 168,
172, 183, 190
chiropractor, xiii, 23, 25, 92
choices, xv, 116, 123, 133,
176, 177
cigarettes, 72
clairaudient, 44
commitment, 51, 84, 139
communication, 154
concentrate, 14, 62, 85
concentrating, 28, 49, 51, 91
concrete people, 3
conviction, 184
copy-cats, 42
crutches, 69
culture, 9

D

D. D. Palmer, 183

H

I

J

K

ABOUT THE AUTHOR

Donald McDowall was born in Australia and is a second-generation chiropractor practicing in Canberra, Australia. He has conducted a private practice since graduation from Palmer College of Chiropractic (Iowa, USA) in 1974. He is a Diplomate of the National Board of Chiropractic Examiners and a Member of the International Board of Applied Kinesiology since 1978. He has continually served in leadership positions of his profession as well as community organisations.

Dr McDowall's interest in healing has led to the publishing of two books about the spiritual aspects of life: *Psychic Surgery – The Philippines Experience* (1993) and *Healing – Doorway to the Spiritual World* (1988). His interest in nutrition and commonsense led to a collection of his advice published in *Clinical Pearls for Better Health* (2002). Music as a component of healing led to him producing a collection of 1920's ragtime Chiropractic songs found on his peer-reviewed, award-winning website http://www.chiroclinic.com.au. Humour is an essential part of healing and has led to Dr McDowall publishing *Wisecracks & Funny Bones – Fun With the Chiropractor* (2003).

Dr McDowall's interest in the subtleties of healing has caused him to explore and gather information from many parts of the world. He has lectured in the United States, Europe, New Zealand and Australia.

Dr. McDowall has been active in community service as well as leadership roles in his profession. He lectures internationally about his specialty practice in Applied Kinesiology and has published papers of clinical interest in professional journals.

Dr McDowall and his wife, Annie, have nine children.

Made in the USA
Lexington, KY
19 August 2017